BLACKSTONE
GUIDE 1

# Living in
# SPAIN

# BLACKSTONE FRANKS GUIDE TO
# Living in
# SPAIN

## SECOND EDITION

KOGAN
PAGE

# Note

This book has been prepared based on the laws of the UK and Spain as at 1 January 1989, and includes the UK Budget proposals of 14 March 1989. It is a general guide only and, in explaining complex matters in a simple way, cannot be relied upon as a substitute for professional advice. The authors and publishers cannot accept any responsibility for loss occasioned to any persons acting (or refraining from action) as a result of reading this book. You must take detailed professional advice relevant to your particular circumstances before any action is taken.

First published in Great Britain in 1988 by
Kogan Page Limited, 120 Pentonville Road,
London N1 9JN

**British Library Cataloguing in Publication Data**

Blackstone Franks guide to living in
   Spain. - 2nd ed
   1. Spain. Tax avoidance
   I. Blackstone Franks & Co.
   336.2'06

   ISBN 0-7494-0007-2

Typeset by DP Photosetting, Aylesbury, Bucks
Printed and bound in Great Britain by
Richard Clay, The Chaucer Press, Bungay

# TRAVEL LIGHT

## Leave your financial worries behind

One of the heaviest burdens to carry, whether you are retiring or working overseas, is the problem of ensuring that your investment, taxation and income situation is dealt with to your best advantage.

Most importantly, if you are retiring overseas you need to know that your capital will provide a realistic level of income, together with real capital growth to protect against inflation in the longer term. If you are working overseas it may be that investment planning and short term tax-breaks should be your principal areas of concern.

As one of the UK's leading independent financial advisers, Blackstone Franks Plc, specialises in providing a wide range of financial services for those who are working or retiring abroad.

For an impartial evaluation of how your income and capital may be put to best use, please request a Confidential Questionnaire from the address below. We will then be able to provide you with an objective assessment and hopefully the answer to your particular financial needs.

## Blackstone Franks

Blackstone Franks Barbican House 26-34 Old Street London EC1V 9HL
Telephone 01-250 3300 Fax 01-250 1402

(FIMBRA)

In *Spain contact* Blackstone Franks Plc Daoiz y Velarde, No 6
Edificio Beneco 2ª y 3ª Apartado de Correos 159 29640 Fuengirola (Malaga)
Tel: (952) 470400 Telex: 79697 Acra E Fax: 476246

# Other Books by Blackstone Franks

Blackstone Franks are a firm of chartered accountants and investment managers with offices in London and Spain.

**Blackstone Franks Guide to Living in Portugal**, Kogan Page
**Working and Retiring Abroad – A Financial Guide**, Blackstone Franks
**The UK as a Tax Haven**, The Economist Publications Ltd
**UK Tax Savings for the Higher Paid**, The Economist Publications Ltd
**The Economist Guide to the Business Expansion Scheme**, The Economist Publications Ltd
**The Blackstone Franks Good Investment Guide**, Kogan Page
**The Blackstone Franks Guide to Perks From Shares**, Kogan Page
**Tolley's Business Start Up Packs**, Tolleys
**The Economist Guide to Management Buy Outs**, The Economist Publications Ltd
**Crawfords Corporate Finance**, The Economist Publications Ltd
**Raising Finance for Business**, The Economist Publications Ltd
**Property Taxes**, Tolley's
**Anti-Avoidance Provisions**, Tolley's
**Tax Planning for Entertainers**, Longman
**Tax Minimisation Techniques**, Longman
**Fringe Benefits**, Longman

# Contents

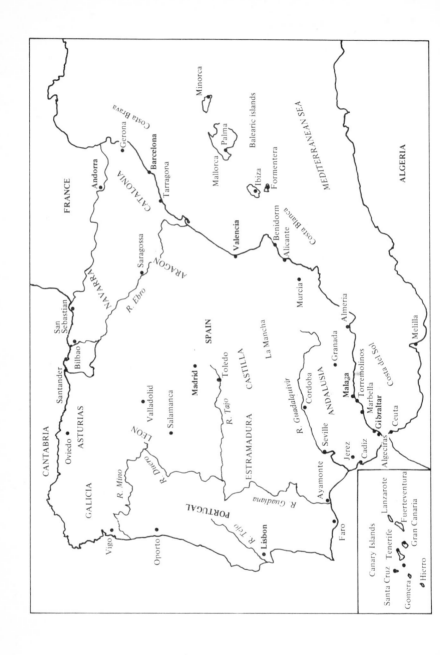

# Introduction

During the past few years increasing numbers of people have gone to live in Spain. The major attractions for those retiring, or going overseas to work, are Spain's cheap housing, good weather and excellent leisure facilities. At the latest estimate there are over a quarter of a million British subjects living in Spain, the European Community's newest member; the trend will undoubtedly continue as communications improve, and the need to understand the complexities of living with both the UK and Spanish tax and legal systems will become more pressing.

Until now there has been little information available to help the newcomers to deal with the laws and regulations they will find in Spain; most people rely on friends for information, but such advice is notoriously poor.

The emigrant's need is for more detailed and accurate information, so that he or she cannot only assess the tax and legal position, but can also choose professional advisers with confidence.

*Blackstone Franks Guide to Living in Spain* is designed to help. It explains clearly the Spanish tax system; the Spanish law on buying a villa or apartment; immigration rules; exchange control laws; work permits; national insurance; the UK tax position on becoming non-resident; and working in Spain and what to do with your UK home.

The book had developed from Blackstone Franks' many years' experience in advising clients moving from the UK to Spain. It answers the innumerable vital questions about such a move: How is UK capital gains tax avoided? Do you have to sell your UK home? What tax is payable in Spain? When can you come back to the UK? What can you do to avoid UK inheritance tax? Does the UK/Spain double tax treaty help? What is the best investment to avoid tax? This book deals with all these problems and many, many more.

Blackstone Franks are the specialists in the UK/Spain rules. This book clarifies those rules, and while it has been written primarily with the new emigrant in mind, it will also prove invaluable to the personal financial adviser who is helping clients with laws which govern a move from the UK to Spain.

This book refers to the Spanish and UK laws as they were known on 1 January 1989, and includes the provisions of the UK Budget of 14 March 1989.

UK: Blackstone Franks Group
Chartered Accountants and Investment Managers
Barbican House
26–34 Old Street
London EC1V 9HL
Tel: 01-250 3300
Fax: 01-250 1402

Spain: Blackstone Franks
Daoiz y Velarde No 6
Edificio Beneco 2ª y 3ª
Apartado de Correos 159
29640 Fuengirola
Malaga
Tel: 010-34-52-479400/462021/461085
Fax: 010-34-52-476246

*Chapter 1*
# Introduction to Spain

## 1.1 Geography

Spain is situated in south-west Europe occupying about 80 per cent of the Iberian peninsula. Its area is 195,000 square miles, making it the largest European country after France. It shares land frontiers with Portugal, France and Andorra. It has 1317 miles of coastline: 712 miles with the Mediterranean to the south and east, and 605 with the Atlantic to the west.

The peninsula comprises an elevated arid tableland surrounded by mountain ranges. The principal rivers are the Duero, the Tajo, the Guadiana, the Guadalquivir, the Ebro and the Miño. The north-west is heavily watered, while the south has lowlands and enjoys a Mediterranean climate. About 40 per cent of the land is arable.

There is a population of 39.6 million (1988 estimate) including an estimated 250,000 Britons. There are believed to be 1 million properties owned by foreigners accommodating about 3 million people, nearly 10 per cent of the population. The population density of 75 per square kilometre compares favourably with 228 for Great Britain. Of EC countries only Greece is less densely populated.

Spain's capital is Madrid. Its main sea port is Barcelona. Barcelona is also Spain's main commercial centre and will host the 1992 Olympic Games.

Spain includes a number of islands. The Balearic Islands are an archipelago off the east coast. The four largest islands are Majorca, Minorca, Ibiza and Formentera. There are seven smaller islands.

The Canary Islands are an archipelago in the Atlantic Ocean off the African coast. It comprises seven islands and six (largely uninhabited) islets.

There are also Isla de Faisanes (an uninhabited Franco-Spanish condominium), Ceuta (a fortified post on the Moroccan coast), and Melilla, a town on a rocky promontory connected to the mainland of Morocco by a narrow isthmus.

Other overseas provinces are now independent countries.

The three main holiday resorts are the *costas*: Costa Brava, Costa del Sol and Costa Blanca. Costa Brava in the north was the original holiday spot when holidaying in Spain became fashionable in the 1950s. Costa del Sol in the south is the most popular area for tourists and retirement. It boasts a hectic social life with plenty of sporting facilities. It is known as the playground of Europe, a term resented by many of its residents.

## 1.2 Climate

The climate of Spain can conveniently be considered in three zones: the Atlantic zone, the Continental zone and the Mediterranean zone. Because of mountain ranges and other factors, it is possible for microclimates to differ from nearby areas.

The Mediterranean zone in the south is the hottest part of the country. The average day temperature can be as high as 34ºC (94ºF) with sunshine for 13 hours a day. Catalonia has mild winters but is also quite humid (between 20 and 31 inches of rain a year); summers avoid excessively high temperatures while having plenty of sunshine (2450 to 2650 hours a year). Valencia and Murcia have a better winter climate, less rain (between 12 and 16 inches a year) and more sunshine (2700 to 3000 hours a year) but summer temperatures can be very high. Andalucia (including the Costa del Sol) has even less rain (9 to 18 inches a year), more sunshine (2900 to 3000 hours a year) and even higher temperatures.

The Atlantic zone in the north-west is cooler, but still warmer than Britain. It rains about one day in three and enjoys less than five hours' sunshine a day, even in August. Galicia particularly has a mild climate. Rias Bajas (near Vigo) enjoys 2400 hours of sunshine a year.

The Continental zone (mainly in the north-east) is cold in winter but boasts the hottest temperatures in summer. Places like Barcelona and Sitges boast temperatures over 90ºF in July and August, but quickly become colder from September.

Eastern cities like Valencia, and places like the Costa Blanca, offer equally good summers but are warmer in the winter.

The Canary Islands offer a climate which is almost like a perpetual UK summer but more humid. Winters are mild and summers avoid excessive highs. Rainfall varies from zero to 27 inches a year; sunshine from 2700 to 30000 hours a year.

The Balearic Islands enjoy a Mediterranean climate but are cooled by sea breezes.

In buying a property, its construction as regards the climate should be considered. For example, a tiled roofed building may look pretty and be comfortable in spring, but will be far too hot and stuffy in summer.

Another climatic consideration is the water supply. Spain has enough natural water supply but has yet to administer it well enough to guarantee no shortages. The problem arises because the municipalities control the supply, and plans to lay national pipelines get frustrated by local issues. See also Section 2.11.

## 1.3 History

Spain has been inhabited from earliest times. It was conquered by Rome in 200 BC, and in the fifth century overrun by the (Christian) Visigoths, and (in 711 AD) African muslims. The Christians reconquered it, and the nation of Spain was formed in 1469 when the kingdoms of Aragon and Castile were united. Its importance grew in the sixteenth century when it founded an Empire.

The War of the Spanish Succession (1701–14) established the Bourbon succession. This has been interrupted four times: between 1808 and 1814 when Napoleon made his brother the king; the first republic between 1873 and 1874; a brief military dictatorship in 1923; and the second republic from 1931 to 1975.

The second republic, formed in 1931 when Alfonso XIII left the country, was largely socialist. In 1936 a military-based counter-revolution broke out. This led to a full civil war which lasted for three years, killing 1 million people. General Franco seized full control on 29 March 1939 and led a right-wing Nationalist government until his death on 20 November 1975. Spain was officially neutral in the two world wars, though, in practice, it supported the fascist countries during the second.

In 1969 Franco appointed Alfonso XIII's grandson, Prince Juan Carlos de Bourbon, as his successor. He became head of state as king Juan Carlos in 1975 and introduced a new democratic constitution in 1978. Under the constitution the head of government is the prime minister who presides over a cabinet. The first free elections were held in June 1977.

The first prime minister was Carlos Arias Navarro. His appointment was followed by widespread demonstrations and industrial strife, leading to his replacement by Adolfo Suárez. In 1982 Spain elected a socialist government under Felipe González.

Spain became a member of the United Nations in 1955, a political member of NATO in 1982 and a member of the EC in 1986. Like all

EC countries Spain must dismantle all frontiers to EC trade and employment by 1992.

Spain has an adequate army, navy and air force.

An attempted military coup on 23 February 1981 failed when most of the army stayed loyal to the king.


## 1.4 Government

Under the 1978 constitution, the country is run by a bicameral parliament known as the Cortes. This comprises a Congress of Deputies, *Congreso de Diputados*, elected every four years by universal adult suffrage, and a Senate of directly elected representatives from the provinces, islands and regions. The last elections were held in 1986.

The prime minister, *presidente*, is proposed by the king to parliament who ratify the appointment. The prime minister forms a cabinet. The current prime minister is Felipe González of the PSOE (socialist party).

There are 17 autonomous regions with their own parliaments and governments: Andalucia, Aragon, Asturias, Balearics, Basque country, Canaries, Castilla-La Mancha, Castilla-Leon, Cantabria, Catalonia, Estremadura, Galicia, Madrid, Murcia, Navarra, La Rioja and Valencia. Some regions, however, want full independence, and the Basque region in particular has been hit by terrorism designed to achieve that aim.

There is also the constitutional court, *El Tribunal Constitucional*, which checks that laws passed by the Cortes are in accordance with the constitution. A council of state, *El Consejo de Estado*, is a government consultative body.

Local authorities take the form of municipalities. They are funded by a mixture of local taxes and state grants. Council members are elected every four years; the last elections were in June 1987. The council then elects a mayor, *alcalde*, deputy mayors, *tenientes de alcalde*, and other members to specific responsibilities.

Foreigners may not vote in national elections (at least not until they have taken Spanish nationality). However, since 1985 they have been able to vote in municipal elections provided their country offers similar rights to Spanish nationals (the UK does).


## 1.5 Language

Spanish is actually a collection of languages, of which the commonest is Castilian, spoken by about three-quarters of the population. Castilian Spanish is the third commonest world language, after Mandarin Chinese and English. It is spoken by about 300 million people worldwide, more than three times the number who speak French.

Basque (believed to be the original language of the Iberian peninsula) is still spoken in the rural districts of Vizcaya, Guipuzcoa and Alava. Catalan is spoken in Provençal Spain. Galician (similar to Portuguese) is spoken in the north-west provinces. Franco discouraged the use of these minority languages, but the present government encourages them.

Spain has a large and rich literature dating from the twelfth century. Its golden age of literature was in the seventeenth century.

Conversational Spanish often proves a problem to the British. It is spoken much faster than British people usually expect. As with our own language, there are local dialects. They are particularly noticeable in the south.

The Spanish alphabet does not use the letter *w*. The symbols *ch* and *ll* are alphabetically placed after *c* and l respectively; thus in an alphabetical listing *pecho* (chest) will follow *pecunia* (cash), and *pillo* (petty thief) follows *pilongo* (dried chestnut). The consonants *b* and *v* are pronounced the same.

If you have to spell words out, to be understood it is necessary to use the Spanish system, which is:

| | | | | | | | |
|---|---|---|---|---|---|---|---|
| A: | Antonio | G: | Gerona | M: | Madrid | T: | Tarragona |
| B: | Barcelona | H: | Historia | N: | Navarra | U: | Ulises |
| C: | Carmen | I: | Inés | O: | Oviedo | V: | Valencia |
| CH: | Chocolate | J: | José | P: | Paris | W: | Washington |
| D: | Dolores | K: | Kilo | Q: | Querido | X: | Xiquina |
| E: | Enrique | L: | Lorenzo | R: | Ramón | Y: | Yegua |
| F: | Francia | LL: | Llobregat | S: | Sábado | Z: | Zaragoza |

### 1.6 Currency

The Spanish unit of currency is the peseta, worth about ½p. The usual abbreviation for pesetas is 'pta' or 'pt', sometimes denoted by the symbol Pt. The peseta used to be divided into 100 céntimos, but these have long since disappeared.

Like other European currencies, the peseta has floated against other currencies since 1972.

Spain maintains very strict exchange control regulations (see Chapter 5) which involves classification of pesetas into different types, particularly the internal peseta (see Section 2.5).

Recent exchange rates are given below:

| | |
|---|---|
| 26 August 1989: | £1 = 192 ptas |
| 31 January 1988: | £1 = 201 ptas |
| 30 September 1987: | £1 = 199 ptas |
| 31 March 1987: | £1 = 205 ptas |
| 31 August 1986: | £1 = 199 ptas |

## 1.7 Trade

The country is fertile and produces heat-loving fruits such as olives, citrus fruits, bananas, apricots, tomatoes, peppers and grapes. Its main cereal is rice, but it also produces wheat, barley, oats, hemp and flax. Spain boasts the highest crop yields (48 to 56 cwt per acre) in the world. The country is the largest provider of olive oil in the world.

It has a large fishing industry based on the Cantabrian and Atlantic coasts. Much of the catch is canned. Fish comprises a major part of the Spanish diet.

Jerez in the south-west is famous for sherry. Spain also has thriving industries in wine (the world's third largest producer), forestry (mainly cork) and livestock.

Most of the country's easily accessible mineral resources have now been exhausted, but efforts are being made to extract less commercial deposits.

The manufacturing industry produces steel, cars, ships, textiles, chemicals, leather goods, ceramics, sewing machines and bicycles.

Spain's principal exports are cars, iron ore, cork, salt, fruit and vegetables, wines and sherry, olive oil, mercury, potash, tinned fruit, tomatoes and footwear. Its principal imports are cotton, cellulose, timber, coffee and cocoa, tobacco, fertilisers, dyes, machinery, cars and tractors, and wool.

The Spanish government seeks to encourage tourism by providing comfortable state-run hotels, known as *paradores*, often in old monasteries and castles and by offering generous concessions to tourists. It is an extremely profitable element in the Spanish economy earning as much as 1.4 trillion pesetas in 1985, and increasing steadily since. Tourism provides over 21 per cent of Spain's foreign earnings, a higher share than in any other country. The number of visitors to Spain increased from 3 million in 1960 to 50.5 million in 1987, of whom 11 million were French, 7.5 million British and 6.6 million German. The Spanish government is

becoming increasingly concerned about the pressures these spiral-
ling numbers are creating, and future promotional plans are taking
this concern into account. Spain hopes to attract more 'quality
tourists' from now on.

America, Canada and Japan are seen as providing the kind of
better-off educated visitor who will travel to the historical and
cultural centres of Spain, rather than spending all his or her time –
and not as much money – on the coastal strip. The season will
become longer, taking in June and September and October; the
department responsible for promoting tourism has spent 1600
million pesetas in the first few months of 1989 promoting Spain in
the foreign media, 100 million of this sum in Japan.

1992 will be a record-breaking year for Spanish tourism. The
Olympics in Barcelona, and a major exhibition in Seville, will bring
hundreds of thousands more visitors to Spain, a prospect which has
forced improvements to Spain's transport and communications
systems and the construction of even more hotels.

Tourism continues to boom as Spain's most successful industry,
but the government is concerned to ensure that the uncontrolled
expansion of 20 years ago is not repeated; there is in Spain, as
elsewhere, a new understanding of the environmental costs
involved.

## 1.8 Economy

The economy under Franco was generally stagnant until the 1960s;
from 1946 to 1950 Spain was subject to a trade boycott. From 1961

**Table 1**   *Rate of real growth 1985–87*

|  | 1985 % | 1986 % | 1987* % | 1987† % |
|---|---|---|---|---|
| Total consumption | 2.3 | 3.7 | 2.9 | 3.4 |
| private | 1.8 | 3.6 | 3.0 | 3.5 |
| public | 4.4 | 4.0 | 2.5 | 3.0 |
| Gross capital formation | 3.9 | 12.0 | 7.8 | 9.0 |
| Domestic demand | 2.7 | 5.2 | 4.0 | 4.5 |
| Exports | 2.9 | 1.1 | 3.7 | 2.5 |
| Imports | 5.4 | 16.0 | 8.6 | 11.0 |
| GDP at market prices | 2.2 | 3.0 | 3.0 | 2.5 |

\* *Official forecasts*
† *Blackstone Franks*
*Source: Contabilidad Nacional de España (INE); Banco de España.*

there was a marked improvement with the development of the machinery, motor and chemical industries. Spain was generally unaffected by the recession of the 1970s but suffered high rates of inflation similar to the UK and Europe.

The inflation rate at the end of 1988 was 7.8 per cent. However, the introduction of VAT on 1 January 1986 (when Spain joined the EC) added 2.8 per cent. By January 1987 it had fallen to 6 per cent. The government aims to bring it to below 5 per cent. Inflation is actually higher than the official figure, as the government omits many items commonly found in the domestic budget.

### 1.9 Education

All children aged between 6 and 15 are guaranteed free education. Private schools provide 30 per cent of primary and 80 per cent of secondary education. They receive government funds if they meet certain criteria.

Education is compulsory between the ages of 6 and 15, though readily available before and after this range. The management of the schools involves teachers, parents and sometimes the students themselves.

The state education is conducted, not unreasonably, only in Spanish. For mature students whose Spanish is inadequate, there are private schools where teaching is in English. Details of such schools can be obtained from the National Association of British Schools in Spain, Arga 9 (El Viso), Madrid 2.

In practice many British residents of Spain send their older children to British schools. Children starting education in Spain are often sent to Spanish schools. Children have no problem becoming fluent in Spanish from school and fluent in English at home.

Nursery education, though not compulsory, is common even in villages. Usually a school bus service is also provided.

The country has 29 state universities and two private universities. The oldest (state) university is Salamanca, founded in 1230.

The country boasts a high literacy rate of 97 per cent.

### 1.10 Diplomatic relations

The UK enjoys full diplomatic relations with Spain. A full list of embassies and consulates is given in Appendix 1.

The main thorn in the flesh of Anglo-Spanish relations concerns Gibraltar which has been under British sovereignty since 1704.

Franco sealed Gibraltar from the Spanish mainland in 1969, but the link was fully re-opened in 1985.

In 1987 an EC package reforming air travel arrangements was vetoed by Spain, solely over their claimed rights to Gibraltar Airport.

## 1.11 Religion

Spain has been a largely Roman Catholic country since 1492. The 1931 constitution disestablished the church and secularised education. Today freedom of religious expression is guaranteed by the constitution.

The Spanish constitution guarantees that children will receive religious and moral education in accordance with their parents' religious convictions.

Religious festivals are celebrated with many colourful local traditions, often including folk dancing and processions. The feast of Corpus Christi (second Thursday after Whitsun) is celebrated by carpeting the streets with flowers. Many towns and villages have their local saints, whose days are also treated as a holiday and festival. There are wide variations between the regions in the nature of celebrations.

Holy Week (the week before Easter) sees the most fervent demonstrations of religious zeal with extended processions in most areas. The most spectacular Holy Week procession is in Seville. The villagers of Catalonia are famous for re-enacting the passion of Christ with great drama and conviction.

Christmas is observed as a religious festival when employers, and sometimes friends, traditionally give hampers. The main exchange of presents is on *Los Reyes*, Epiphany (6 January). On Epiphany there is a special Twelfth Night cake, the *roscón*. It is traditional to welcome a New Year by eating 12 grapes outdoors.

The patron saint of Spain is St James the Great, credited with first preaching the gospel in Spain.

## 1.12 Culture and leisure

There is more to Spanish culture than many tourists see.

Spain boasts many buildings of great architectural interest, particularly among its churches and castles. But even the humblest town or village usually has its charms. Every town and village has its *plaza mayor* or main square, often with a covered arcade leading to it. The square is usually an extended forecourt of the town or village hall.

The country is also famous for its furniture (particularly chests); tapestries and embroideries; gold, silver and iron work (including wrought iron screens); sculpture; and ceramics (including *azulejos*, glazed pottery tiles).

It has consistently produced painters of note from the tenth century. In this century the 'Paris School' has produced such internationally known names as Salvador Dali and Pablo Picasso.

Composers such as Enrique Granados, Isaac Albeniz, Manuel de Falla and Joaquin Rodrigo have gained international recognition. Spain has also produced some eminent musicians including the guitarist Andrés Segovia, and the cellist Pablo Casals.

The cinema is the most popular form of entertainment.

Spain also has a form of entertainment peculiar to itself, the *zarzuela*, a musical play with spoken passages, songs and dances. In Andalucia, displays of the flamenco dance are also very popular.

The national sport is football which has a greater national following in Spain than in Britain. The most popular teams are Real Madrid and Atlético. Other sports have more local followings, such as *pelota* in the Basque country, and water sports and skiing in the north-west. People gamble on the football results through the *quiniela* or tote.

Cafés provide the centre of social activity in the town and village. The lunchtime break (from 1 pm) is known as *chateo*, and the evening break the *tertulia*.

Spain has many culinary delights. These include *churros* (twisted fritters) and *horchata de chufas* (a cold drink made from almonds). Many regions have their own specialities, such as *gazpacho*, a cold tomato and cucumber soup which is a speciality of Andalucia.

Caravanning is popular in Spain, which has many camp sites, particularly in the south. Full details are available from the Spanish National Tourist Office. They provide a camping map, *Mapa de campings españoles*, free. An International Camping Carnet may be obtained from the AA or RAC for £2.50 on production of a photograph. This is accepted at most camp sites in lieu of a passport.


## 1.13 Working conditions

Chapter 6 gives information about working and employing people in Spain.

Spain has 15 national public holidays. These are:

| | |
|---|---|
| 1 January (New Year's Day) | 25 July |
| 6 January (Epiphany) | 15 August |
| 19 March | 12 October |
| Maundy Thursday | 1 November |
| Good Friday | 6 December |
| 1 May | 8 December |
| Corpus Christi (2nd Thursday | 24 December |
| after Whitsun) | 25 December |

In addition each town has a public holiday for its own patron saint.

Office and shop hours are usually from 9 or 9.30 am to about 1.30 pm, and then from 3.30 to 7.30 pm. Banks are open from 9 am to 2 pm on weekdays and from 9 am to 1 pm on Saturdays. There is a move afoot away from the two-hour siesta to a standard lunch break.

Many UK settlers find the general pace of life slower than in Britain. Promises that something will be fixed 'tomorrow' (*mañana*) often need a generous interpretation of 'tomorrow'.

Spain is notorious for certain unconventional practices, hence the expression 'Spanish customs' (see section 2.6 for example). However, in fairness it must be said that efforts are being made to correct these, and have been particularly successful in the field of tax (see Section 3.1).

## 1.14 Law

Spanish law is based on Napoleonic law, which in turn is based on Roman law. It differs from English law in many important respects; for example, it does not recognise trusteeship.

All laws must be formulated in accordance with the Spanish constitution of 1981. A constitutional court can strike out or amend a law which it finds as unconstitutional, and has done so in the case of the law of foreigners (Section 4.5).

Spanish law recognises the usual criminal offences and civil arrangements, such as contracts. The law has become more akin to UK law in recent years. Spain is a signatory to the United Nations Declaration on Human Rights and to the European Court of Justice.

The courts, however, operate on the inquisitorial system common on the Continent, rather than the adversarial system used in Britain. Residents who are not Spanish nationals and who commit serious offences are subject to deportation (discussed further in Section 4.5).

Spanish courts are as slow and inefficient as anyone else's. They range from the justice of the peace, *juzgado de la paz*, through the provincial court, *Audiencia Provincial*, to the constitutional court.

The diagram below shows the structure of Spain's law courts system.

The functions of the different courts are as follows:

1 *Juzgados de Distrito/Juzgados de Paz*
There is one in each judicial district. They deal with offences and will become *Juzgados de Primera Instancia* in the impending judicial reorganisation.

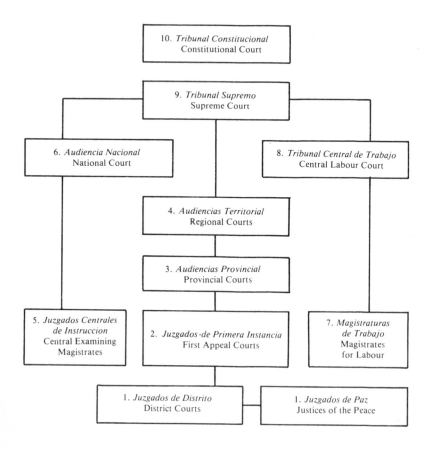

**Figure 1** *Structure of Spanish law court system*

2 *Juzgados de Primera Instancia*
These are first appeal courts, located in all provincial capitals and other important cities.

3 *Audiencias Provincial*
These are provincial courts. There is one in each province, dealing with criminal cases.

4 *Audiencias Territorial*
These are regional courts. After the reorganisation they will be called higher courts and there will be one in each autonomous region of Spain. They will deal with both civil and criminal cases.

5 *Juzgados Centrales de Instruccion* (Central Examining Magistrates)
These courts examine cases which have a national dimension or which affect more than one regional court.

6 *Audiencia Nacional* (National Court)
This court hands down judgments in national cases of a criminal, administrative or labour nature.

7. *Magistraturas de Trabajo* (Magistrates for Labour Matters)
These courts are organised by provinces and deal only with labour questions.

8. *Tribunal Central de Trabajo* (Central Labour Court)
This court passes judgments on cases examined by magistrates for labour matters. It will disappear after the reorganisation.

9 *Tribunal Supremo* (Supreme Court)
The highest court in the land.

Civil actions start with a *demanda*. A complaint may be made by a *denuncia* registered with the police, from which criminal proceedings may result.

There are other ways to complain. Often a call to the consulate or the town hall can resolve a problem. Section 2.1 advises on what to do if property deals go wrong.

Spanish laws on specific topics are given elsewhere in this book:

employment, investment and trading: Chapter 6;
exchange control: Chapter 5;
property: Chapter 2;
tax: Chapter 3;
wills: Section 1.15.

It is a legal requirement that people must carry personal identification on them at all times. For British residents that will usually be a passport or residence permit.

Provisions regarding family law are given below.

All births in Spain must be registered at the Civil Registry (usually at the town hall) within eight days, regardless of the status of the parents. Non-resident British nationals should obtain a full birth certificate and register the birth at the British consulate. From 1 January 1983 a child born in Spain whose mother or father is British by birth assumes British nationality. If neither is British by birth but one is otherwise a British citizen, the baby may obtain British nationality on proof that at least one parent lived in Britain for three years before the birth. The baby will have Spanish nationality if one parent is Spanish or if born out of wedlock and the father is not identified. Spain does not recognise dual nationality for adults (though Britain does) so the child will have to choose his nationality between the ages of 18 and 19.

Marriage in church is permitted only if at least one party is a Roman Catholic. Anglican churches in Spain are forbidden to take marriages. For a church wedding, the couple must first prove before a judge that they are single and of age. The priest usually arranges the other formalities, including calling banns. If only one party is a Roman Catholic, special permission for the marriage is needed from the church authorities. Civil weddings take place before a judge of the Civil Registry. All marriages must be registered at the Civil Registry. Britons may marry at a British consulate or in Gibraltar.

Marriages may be ended by divorce, separation and nullity. Since 15 August 1981 Spain has modelled its divorce laws on those generally followed in Europe (including the UK) whereby divorce is possible when it can be shown that the marriage has irretrievably broken down. Divorce is only possible after one year of marriage.

Deaths must be registered promptly at the Civil Registry. Whoever registers the death must have a death certificate signed by a doctor stating the cause of death. For a British subject, the death certificate should also be taken to the British consulate which will issue a British death certificate.

There is no need for anyone living in Spain to take Spanish nationality. You may elect to do so after you have lived in Spain for ten years. You have to swear allegiance to the Spanish crown and renounce your former nationality. British nationality can only be renounced on formal application to the Foreign Office. There is also much paperwork involved in becoming a Spanish national. As a Spanish national, you are treated as if you were a native Spaniard. You may vote, stand for public office and you can become liable for military service.

## 1.15 Wills

What happens to your estate when you die depends on your will (if any) and the laws of two countries. Although the rules are complex, in practice if you make adequate provision for your immediate family in a will drafted under either country's laws, there should not be a problem. For completeness the detailed provisions are given below.

If a British national dies in Spain, his estate will generally be distributed according to his British will. The exception is that his immovable property (ie real estate) in Spain may only be distributed according to Spanish law, which differs markedly from UK law.

If you have taken out Spanish nationality, your whole estate will be administered under Spanish law.

Spanish law recognises certain relations as 'obligatory heirs', *heredores forzosos*, to whom part of the estate must pass. These are the spouse and children, grandchildren or remoter descendants (surviving issue).

If a person dies leaving a husband or wife, the surviving spouse is entitled to keep all assets acquired before marriage, half the assets acquired during marriage, and all personal gifts (including other inheritances). These items do not form part of the deceased's estate.

The other half of the estate is divided into three equal shares. One-third of this part (one-sixth of the whole) passes to the children equally. Another third passes to the children as directed by the will but with a life interest to the spouse. The last third passes to anyone as directed by the will. If there is no will, this share passes to the children equally. If a child has already died, his or her share passes to the child's own children.

Foreigners may make wills in Spain regardless of their nationality, residence or domicile. There are three types: the commonest is the open will, *testamento abierto*, a copy of which is filed centrally; a closed (secret) will, *testamento cerrado*; or a holograph will (in your handwriting) which has to be authenticated before a judge before becoming admissible. These wills are usually drafted for you by a lawyer, but do not have to be. It is even possible to make a verbal will before five witnesses, though this is not advised.

It cannot be stressed too strongly, though, that you should always have a valid will. Although there is a temptation to regard the lawyer's fees as a waste of money, particularly when your wishes are simple, both Spanish and English law attach specific meanings to certain phrases which can defeat your actual intentions. For example, a bequest 'to all my grandchildren' may have to be frozen until your daughters and daughters-in-law are past childbearing age to ensure that there are no more grandchildren to whom it can be distributed.

Under Spanish law the assets of the deceased may only be distributed when any Spanish inheritance tax has been paid. If the tax is not paid within six months of death, interest starting at 10 per cent is added. A Spanish lawyer should be contracted as soon as possible after the death.


## 1.16 Practical points

Spain has an ombudsman who deals with all complaints concerned with officialdom. The system seems to work well and has been widely used by foreigners. It has been observed that the prime minister and the ombudsman answer letters more promptly and thoroughly than most town mayors and local officials.

Spain uses the metric system of units entirely. Conversion of clothes sizes from Spanish to British measures are given in Table 2.

Spain is one hour ahead of Greenwich Mean Time.

The electricity supply in Spain is 220 or 225 volts AC, but may be 110 volts in parts of the Balearic Islands.

Hotels, cafés and restaurants include service charges in their bills. Sometimes a boy will offer to carry your bag or help to see your car out of a car park. He expects a tip for doing so.

Cafés and restaurants are obliged by law to keep a complaint sheet, *hoja de reclamación*, to record all customers' complaints. The sheet is sent to an inspector.

The crime rate has steadily increased in recent years and is now about the same as for other north European countries. Spain is also fighting a drug problem as narcotics are smuggled in from North Africa. Adequate security must always be considered, particularly in remote locations.

Social attitudes have become much more liberal, even permitting topless bathing at certain popular resorts. Certainly the days when miniskirted tourists got into trouble are over.

Cars drive on the right-hand side of the road. Drivers must give way to traffic from the right. Wearing seat belts is compulsory. Cars must carry a red warning triangle to display in the event of a breakdown. The petrol sold is 'super' (97 octane) and 'normal' (92 octane); however, supplies can be hard to find in rural areas. Diesel is also available.

Provisions regarding driving licences are given in Section 4.6.

**Table 2**   *Conversion of clothes sizes from Spanish to British measures*

| Men's shirts | | Men's suits | |
|---|---|---|---|
| *Spanish* | *British* | *Spanish* | *British* |
| 36 | 14 | 46 | 36 |
| 37 | 14½ | 48 | 38 |
| 38 | 15 | 50 | 40 |
| 39 | 15½ | 52 | 42 |
| 40 | 16 | 54 | 44 |
| 41 | 16 | 56 | 46 |
| 42 | 16½ | 58 | 48 |
| 43 | 17 | 60 | 50 |
| 44 | 17½ | | |

| Men's shoes | | Men's socks | |
|---|---|---|---|
| *Spanish* | *British* | *Spanish* | *British* |
| 39 | 5 | 38 | 9 |
| 40 | 6 | 39 | 9½ |
| 41 | 7 | 40 | 10 |
| 42 | 8 | 41 | 10½ |
| 43 | 9 | 42 | 11 |
| 44 | 10 | 43 | 11½ |
| 45 | 10½ | 44 | 12 |
| 46 | 11 | | |
| 47 | 12 | | |
| 48 | 13 | | |

| Ladies' dresses | | Ladies' shoes | |
|---|---|---|---|
| *Spanish* | *British* | *Spanish* | *British* |
| 38 | 8 | 35 | 2 |
| 40 | 10 | 36 | 3 |
| 42 | 12 | 37 | 4 |
| 44 | 14 | 38 | 5 |
| 46 | 16 | 39 | 6 |
| 48 | 18 | 40 | 7 |
| 50 | 20 | 41 | 8 |

Petrol stations are owned by the government; they do not accept credit cards.

The country is partly served by motorways, though some popular parts remain fairly inaccessible. Most motorways are subject to a toll.

Taxis are widely used in Spain. It is quite normal to take a taxi from Barcelona airport to Valencia, 300 miles away.

Spain has Europe's smallest number of telephones; per 100 of the population, Spain has 25 telephones. Telephones in Spain are served by an automatic service which links with most of the rest of the world. To ring Spain from the UK you dial 01034 immediately followed by the full Spanish telephone number omitting the first digit. To ring the UK from Spain you dial 07 and wait for a loud continuous tone. You then dial 44 followed by the full UK number, but omitting the first digit (usually 0). So to dial 01-250 3300 from Spain, you would dial 07, wait for the tone, then 441-250 3300. When dialling within Spain, you dial only the exchange number if calling another number within the same province, and the whole number (with the provincial code) if calling another exchange.

If you are lucky enough to have a telephone, you can pay the bill directly by going to the local offices of Telefonica (Spain's equivalent of BT) or you can arrange a standing order with your bank. To do this you must first inform Telefonica by letter of your intention, telling them the name and address of your bank, the number of your account and telephone number. Send a copy of this letter to your bank.

The phone company will use various terms on the bill; these are most important:

1 *Facturation.* This is the period for which you are being billed.
2 *Total a Pajon* This means the total you must pay.
3 *Custno de Abono* is the standing charge for the line and the telephone(s) you have.
4 *Servicio Lectua* is the number of *pasos* (basic tariff units) you have used.
5 *Base Imponible* is the preliminary total, to which 12 per cent IVA (VAT) is added.

Your telephone bill must be paid within 20 days, or Telefonica will suspend the service.

Pollution has been a major problem. Major improvements have been made in the last ten years in treating sewage and in better rubbish collection. However, there are still some black spots.

The open seasons for freshwater fishing are:

salmon: first Sunday in March to 18 July (limit: 3 fish a day);
trout: first Sunday in March to 15 August (limit: 20 fish a day);
high mountain trout: 16 May to 30 September;
sturgeon: 1 January to 31 July;
river crab: Thursdays, Saturdays and public holidays between 21
    June and 31 August.

Sea fishing is permitted all year from one hour before dawn to one hour after sunset.

Hunting is permitted from mid-September to mid-February. Only the lynx is a protected species, though there are restrictions on certain types of bear. That leaves the deer, mountain goat (including ibex), roebuck, boar, wolf and mountain sheep. Small game hunting is permitted all year. You must have a hunting licence and comply with the laws regarding firearms.

Most British flowers and shrubs will bloom in Spain, usually for much longer than at home. Roses, for example, can be picked for most of the year. In addition, it is also possible to grow shrubs such as mimosa and hibiscus.

The Spanish fly is a beetle which provides the main source of cantharidin, which was once commonly used as a blistering agent and diuretic.

## 1.17 The police and your rights

You cannot be arbitrarily held by the police, though they can arrest you without a warrant if they have reasonable grounds to believe you have committed an arrestable offence. You must be read your constitutional rights (in Spanish) before they take you away. You can be held for three days before you are taken to a judge, though the judge must be informed of your arrest within 24 hours. You have the right to make the police contact your lawyer, though you cannot make the call yourself. If the police have no solid charges against you, they will probably release you within the 24-hour limit.

## 1.18 Buying or selling a car

Buying or selling a used car in Spain can be a hazardous business, but if you take care to ensure that all the necessary paperwork is completed to cover yourself against liabilities, things should go smoothly. Any Spanish car must have two documents: a *Permiso de Circulacion*, which makes it legal to drive the car on public roads, and a *Tarjeta de Inspeccion Technica de Vehiculos* or a Certificate of Roadworthiness. If you buy a car it must have these.

If you sell a car, you must sign the section on the back of the *Permiso de Circulacion* which begins 'Transferido ...'. To make sure no problems arise you should also write in the date of the sale. This obliges the new owner to complete the paperwork within ten days. You can also notify the *Jefatura Provincial de Trafico* of the sale, to cover yourself in case the buyer omits to change the name on the car's papers. If the car is still in your name after the sale, the new owner could be running up fines for which you will be liable. You can check this: ask at the *Jefatura* for the form called *Solicitud de Datos del Registro de Vehiculos* (Request for Vehicle Registration Details). This will tell you whether or not you are still the car's registered owner.

If you are buying a car you must ask the seller for two further documents. The local car tax, *Impuesto Sobre la Circulacion de Vehiculos*, should be fully paid up to date (ask to see the vendor's passport or identity card to check that his or her signature is genuine, and ask for a photocopy for your own security, in case anything goes wrong). The other document you should have is a *Transferencia*. This should be completed and signed, and is obtainable from *Jefatura Provincial de Trafico*. Help with all these papers can be given by a competent *qestor* or by the RACE: *Real Automovil Club de España*.

Be careful to check the legal status of any car you buy. All cars made before 1980 must pass a roadworthiness test, *Inspeccion Technica de Vehiculos* or ITV.

See also Section 4.6 on driving lessons and tourist plates.


### 1.19 Television

BBC-TV Europe began broadcasting to Europe in spring 1989 via the Intelsat V satellite. Eighteen hours of programmes (mostly BBC 1) are broadcast daily, and Spanish residents can tune in with a satellite dish (of at least 1.5 metres for southern Spain) and a BBC-TV Europe decoder which costs 111,000 pesetas. Make sure it carries the official BBC-TV Europe logo and beware of imitations – the BBC is taking steps to ensure that pirate decoders will not work for long. Official distributors for BBC-TV Europe decoders are:

Costa del Sol:   European Electronic Communications SA,

|  | Carolina Park, Ctra de Cadiz Km 178, Marbella (Tel: 952 82869) |
|---|---|
| Others: | Display Communications SA, Sant Pere, 50 (bajo), Gandia (Valencia) RG Ingeneria, Commandante Zonita 6, Madrid (Tel: 91-233 7297) |

Video World is a fortnightly subscription video service. A three-hour video cassette includes a selection of BBC 1 and BBC 2 programmes showing news analysis, sports, features, drama and light entertainment. Subscription rates are £180 for six months, £295 for a year and £585 for two years. Call freefone 0800 44 41 41 in the UK, or write to BBC Video World, 39-40 Skylines, Lime Harbour, London E14 9TS.

## 1.20  Repairs to household machines

There are new rules which protect the consumer when having household machines repaired. The main points are:

- They cover both the 'white' household machines, like fridges, dishwashers and stoves, as well as the 'brown' ones, like televisions, radios and video recorders.
- The guarantee given on household machines lasts a minimum of three months. This guarantee is total, including transport of the machine, of the technicians, parts and materials, wages and even taxes.
- The firm is obliged to give an estimate on any repair unless the client explicitly waives this.
- The estimate must include:
  - the reason for the repair;
  - a diagnosis of the breakdown;
  - the total price with details of materials, wages and the IVA (VAT) of 12 per cent;
  - the date foreseen for finishing the repair.
- The estimate must be given within a maximum of five days after the client asks for it and is valid for 30 days.
- If the client refuses to accept the estimate, he must pay the costs of providing it: for white household machines, 30 minutes' labour costs; for brown machines, 60 minutes' labour costs; and for small apparatus, 15 minutes' labour costs;
- If the client does not collect his machine from the repair shop within 30 days, he will have to pay for storage.

- All spare parts used in repairs must be new. The client has the right to receive the parts replaced, unless it is a guarantee repair.
- Repair shops, *Servicios de Assistencia Technica (SAT)*, must have complaint forms available and display information on prices.

# Chapter 2

# The Legal Side of Buying a Property in Spain

## 2.1 Introduction

Buying property in Spain has become very popular. The country has a beautiful climate, and in recent years has made great efforts to attract tourists and foreign residents. Spain now derives more of its foreign earnings from tourism than any other country. About 250,000 Britons currently live in Spain.

The old disincentives to living in Spain have largely been removed. Since the end of Franco's dictatorship, Spain has established what has proved to be a stable democracy, joined the EC and generally become more like other European countries, while still retaining its own character.

This increased popularity has led to significant rises in property values. Prices of properties near the popular resorts are no longer 'give-away' bargains, but there are still bargains to be had.

As these trends are likely to continue, buying Spanish property can be a good investment. However, as with all residential property, investment as a factor should only be considered after domestic considerations. If you want a more speculative property investment, Portugal probably offers more scope.

Before buying property in Spain, you should visit different areas to see where you wish to settle. Having found your area, you may wish to consider living there experimentally by buying a timeshare from a reputable source. Living in a country is quite a different experience from holidaying in a tourist-oriented resort where you are not particularly concerned with how much you spend. A book such as this can only give general advice; whether living in Spain works for you is something only you can determine.

Sometimes foreigners buy a small property first. These are easier to resell once you have become accustomed to the transition of living in another land and are looking for a permanent residence.

Older property can often be offered at bargain prices, but you should check its structure. It will not have been built to the exacting standards which are compulsory today. Building repairs are

expensive in Spain. It cannot be stressed too strongly that you should use the services of a reputable Spanish lawyer to complete any property transactions. Never sign anything until you have obtained legal advice. Ignore the selling agent's advice; it is not reliable. The British consulate (details given in Section 1.10) will help you in this and many other matters. There is also a list in Appendix 5 of solicitors in the UK specializing in Spanish law.

A popular property is the *finca*, a farmhouse usually 100 years or more old. These can be well built and are very much in demand.

Another practical matter to consider is whether the sewage arrangements are adequate. Some buildings still have cesspits in unhygienic conditions.

If you want a property by the sea, it is often advisable to buy a property a little inland rather than on the beach. Not only will it be cheaper, it will usually be quieter and less humid.

If you buy or are considering buying property, you should consider joining the Institute of Foreign Property Owners, *Instituto de Propetarios Extranjeros*. Their UK address is: 38 Hillfield Road, London NW6 1PZ; 01-431 2499.

If things do go wrong, you can appeal to the ombudsman, *Defensor del Pueblo*. He is elected by parliament to deal with all complaints made by the public. The present ombudsman is Sr Joaquin Ruiz-Jimenez, and his address is: Calle Fortuny 22, 28010 Madrid.

Another source of help is your own Euro-MP, or the Euro-MP for York, Edward McMillan-Scott, who is the 'European Parliament rapporteur on transnational property transactions'.

Assuming you have bought your property without any problem, make sure that you note the addresses and telephone numbers of your local police station and doctor.

## 2.2 Restrictions

Most legal restrictions on British people buying property in Spain have now been removed. Substantial concessions were made in April 1985 when the Gibraltar frontier was re-opened. Restrictions were further relaxed when Spain joined the EC in 1986.

A foreigner now needs simply to notify his purchase to the Ministry of Commerce rather than obtain their permission. The Ministry retains the (rarely used) power to prohibit a purchase.

Of the remaining restrictions, no foreigner is allowed to own more than three flats in the same building. A foreigner needs government permission to buy more than 4 hectares (9.9 acres) of irrigated land or 20 hectares (50 acres) of non-irrigated land. A portion of land exceeding 5000 square metres (1.23 acres) for building a house is classified as a business activity and needs special permission from the Director General of Foreign Transactions.

In the past British settlers have sought to overcome restrictions by using Spanish nationals as nominee owners. This is not to be recommended as it is illegal (with heavy penalties) and means that the British 'owner' has no legal title or rights on the property. Spanish law does not generally recognise nominee ownership as allowed by English law.

Certain rural areas in the islands and parts of mainland Spain have been declared special areas of strategic defence (military zones). Before 1986, a British subject could own property in these areas only with permission of the Army Ministry. Since 1986 EC nationals (including UK nationals) are not restricted in this way, though it is known that problems still exist in parts of Minorca.

### 2.3 Legal title

When a new property is built in Spain, various documents must be registered according to the nature of the property.

Under Article 1280 of the Spanish Civil Code, all Spanish property sales and purchases must be registered in a local deed registry. The conveyance deed is known as the *escritura de compraventa* and is signed by the purchaser and seller.

If you cannot be there in person to sign the *escritura de compraventa*, it is necessary to appoint a special power of attorney. This is known as the *escritura de poder de compraventa*. If a husband and wife are jointly buying the property, they must each either be present or be represented under a power of attorney. The power of attorney must be written in Spanish and may be given by a simple letter or even verbally, but such a power must be ratified within 30 days before a *notario* or Spanish consulate.

An *escritura* may be drawn up by the Spanish Embassy in London, but this takes time as it has to be authenticated in Madrid. It also costs more.

Unlike English law, debt can attach to property. So if your seller is bankrupt or in arrears with the mortgate payments, his creditors or mortgages may exercise their right to take the property, even after you have purchased it.

If you live as a member of a Community (which is common), there are special rules which must be followed (see Section 2.17).

Consideration should be given regarding the names in which the property is to be registered. If registered in your name (or joint names with your husband or wife) you incur a future liability for Spanish inheritance and gift tax and for personal income tax when you sell it. It also creates a potential liability for Spanish inheritance tax on your beneficiaries and can increase any inheritance tax you have to pay on anything you may otherwise inherit, as the rates of Spanish inheritance tax are partly determined according to the wealth of the donee (see Sections 3.13 and 3.14).

An alternative is to register the property in the names of your children with yourself (and husband or wife) as life tenants, *usofructarios*. This, however, has the disadvantage that your options on the property are now severely limited (it is no longer yours). A serious problem, which is often overlooked, is that if your child gets divorced, his or her ex-spouse is entitled to a share of the property. Finally there is always the chance that your children can die before you.

The third choice is to register the property in the name of an offshore company which you control either directly or by an offshore trust, and to name yourself as the beneficiary. This option can be expensive to administer, so the costs of doing it should be balanced against any possible tax savings. See Chapter 14 for more information.

## 2.4 The escritura de compraventa

The *escritura de compraventa* is prepared by a *notario*. The *notario* is a public official who has no real equivalent in the English system. Many of his duties are similar to those of an English solicitor, but he is solely concerned that the legal requirements have been met in full. He does not necessarily act in the best interests of either party. The *notario* has no responsibility to the parties, his job is simply to see that some of the government regulations have been satisfied.

The purchaser should therefore always ensure that he has a Spanish lawyer (known as an *abogado*) to act for him, and that the lawyer is not also acting for the seller. It is not unknown for property to be sold several times without there having been an *escritura* registered. For a new property, the Spanish lawyer will also check at the town hall, *Ayuntamiento*, that the developer has obtained proper planning permission.

Unlike the UK, Spanish lawyers are not compelled to carry personal insurance. Some solicitors have a bond against which a claim can in theory be made, but this is difficult in practice. In Spain, conveyance means just that and no more. There is no legally imposed standard of care.

Another difference from the English system is that one lawyer can act for both parties. This is not recommended in practice.

One of the functions of the *notario* is to see that the relevant exchange control regulations have been followed (see Sections 2.5 and 2.6). For him to legalise the conveyance, he must see:

- a copy of the form TE 13 which is submitted to the Ministry of Commerce (DGTE) with details of the intended purchase duly stamped as approved by them; and
- a certificate from the bank stating that the purchase consideration has been introduced from outside Spain (not necessary if you have a residence permit – see Section 4.3).

If the property is in a military zone, a 'permission to purchase' signed by the Military Governor for the zone must also be produced if the purchase is made by a non-EC national. If the documents are presented by the lawyer, he must also produce a properly notarised power of attorney.

The agreement for sale is known as the *contrato*, or *privato*.

Spanish law does not require there to be a preliminary written agreement but it is advisable. It should, for example, specify that any deposit is returnable.

Articles 1278 and 1279 of the Spanish Civil Code govern private agreements for sale. Such agreements create a legally binding contractual relationship whereby either party can require the other to appear before the *notario* when the price is paid or tendered. This, however, is risky as it does not prevent the seller selling to another buyer or mortgaging the property. Nor does it prevent the seller's creditors making a prior claim on the property. A holder of an *escritura* has better title than the holder of an earlier private contract. The only remedy available to a person so cheated of his property is to start proceedings for fraud.

A search on the property must be made twice: once at the beginning of your enquiries, and again when registering the property. If a property is sold as being free of debt when it is not, a criminal case of fraud can be brought. However, this will achieve little in practice if the fraudster has left the country.

The signing of the conveyance can be several months after conclusion of the private contract. Your lawyer will therefore usually make a last check that the vendor still has a clear title, and that the property has not been mortgaged or charged, or even sold to someone else.

Your title to the property becomes final when details are entered in the property register. This should be done as soon as possible after the *escritura* is signed. Though it is unusual for the purchaser or his lawyer to take the *escritura* straight from the *notario* to the property register, this is not impossible and you should insist on it. If this is not practical, the lawyer can arrange for further inscriptions on the property to be blocked for 60 days.

The property register return your *escritura* to you with their official stamp and inscription reference on it. An *escritura* can be registered even though there is not good title. To ensure that the *escritura* gives good title it must be translated from Spanish and properly checked. This may seem an unnecessary expense, but is essential to guarantee good title to the property. Failure to do this has been a problem for many British buyers.

Only when this document is in your possession and the title has been checked do you have good title to the property. Some Spanish property registers have such a large backlog of work that it can take a year to get the *escritura* back from them.

## 2.5 Internal pesetas

The price stipulated in the *escritura* must be paid in 'internal pesetas'. The *notario* will require a certificate from a Spanish bank that sufficient internal pesetas have been purchased by foreign currency. This condition does not apply if you already have a residence permit (see Section 4.3) or if you buy as a non-resident from another non-resident. However, the condition *does* apply if you buy property through an offshore company.

This purchase is known as a 'foreign money contribution'. It ensures that the pesetas can be exchanged back for sterling should you wish to repatriate your investment.

In practice a non-resident can usually obtain the certificate by telexing funds from abroad (remembering to include a sufficient amount for bank charges) to a convertible peseta account (Section 5.2) in your name. The remitting bank must advise the receiving bank of the name for whom the funds are being transmitted and the purpose of the transmission (eg to purchase Apartment X or Y in Z).

The figure on the bank certificate, the *escritura de compraventa* and the form TE 13 must all be the same, failing which the *notario* will refuse to register the property.

If you do not have and cannot establish a convertible peseta account in Spain, the money may be transmitted to that of a professional adviser. However, you should remember that Spain does not recognise trusteeship as in English law, and that such funds are available to your adviser (and his creditors) without restriction.

Before UK exchange controls were abolished in 1979, internal pesetas attracted an investment currency premium. Some tourists therefore bought their property from other tourists in sterling. This is, and always has been, quite legal, but it should be remembered that such expenditure cannot be easily repatriated, though you could still sell your property to someone else for sterling.

### 2.6 Property taxes and fees

The *notario* charges a registration fee and a fee for his own services. These are calculated according to the registered value (commonly called the 'declared value') of the property. The purchaser is liable to pay the registration fee, and the seller is liable to pay the *notario's* fees, but sometimes the purchaser agrees to pay the latter.

The purchaser is also liable to pay a tax on the transaction. The first tax depends on whether the property is bought privately or from a developer. For a private sale he pays a $5\frac{1}{2}$ per cent transfer tax known as *impuesto sobre transmisiones* (IT), but no VAT.

He pays value added tax known as *impuesto sobre el valor añadido* (IVA) at 12 per cent for a plot of land or community property bought from a developer, and 6 per cent for a property bought privately. In the Canary Islands, the old purchase tax (IGTE) of $4\frac{1}{2}$ per cent is payable.

The seller is liable to pay another tax which is called *arbitrio sobre incremento del valor de los terrenos*, which is more commonly known as the *plus valía*. This is a tax on the land only. It is charged once per ownership on the capital gain during the ownership of the property. The values were revised on 24 May 1984 and are being further revised regularly to bring these values into line with market values. Anyone buying or selling property previously bought before that date should check that the *plus valía* has been adjusted accordingly. Although the seller is liable for this tax, its liability is registered against the property, making the purchaser liable if the seller defaults. Quite often the purchaser agrees to pay this tax.

The *plus valía* is charged at rates between 10 and 40 per cent and can easily become a large sum. The purchaser should be especially careful to check that the vendor has met or will meet this liability. He should also check whether the values entered on the *escritura* are the correct values and not adjusted as a tax fiddle (see below).

The two fees and the IT or IVA are payable soon after the *escritura* is signed, but the *plus valía* is not payable until some months later.

In practice, the seller is often required to pay *todos gastos*, all expenses. This should be remembered when negotiating the price.

In addition to these fees and taxes, the seller should remember that he is liable to pay his own lawyer's fees. These are calculated on the basis of time spent, as with English lawyers. The lawyer will be able to tell you how much all the fees and taxes should be. The figure will usually be in excess of 10 per cent of the purchase price. His own fee is typically about 4 per cent of the price.

Taxes and rates payable once the property has been purchased are discussed in Section 2.9.

A common dodge in Spain was to have two 'purchase prices', the actual purchase price and the 'official price' which is entered on the *escritura*. You will know this is happening if you are asked for two cheques, one for the *escritura* value, perhaps 40 per cent of the actual price, and the balance payable to bearer, *al portador*.

The idea was to avoid transfer tax and it was once regarded as normal practice. However, the tax authorities have tightened up on this in recent years and will simply restate the consideration at market value if they believe that the purchase price was deliberately understated. In serious cases of undervaluation they have the right to buy the property from you at the undervaluation, that is, to seize it. The tax authorities must exercise such an option within two years of the purchase.

The arrangement has the disadvantage that, unless your eventual purchaser makes a similar agreement, your tax bill will be greater on your eventual sale. It can also mean that the undeclared element of the purchase consideration can be left in non-convertible pesetas, which cannot be repatriated (at least not legally).

In 1989 further laws were passed whereby the notaries and registrars can only base their fees on the values declared in the contract, and can be fined or barred from practice if they use two prices. In addition, if the *Hacienda* (tax office) decide that the market value is much higher than the declared value they will:

- charge the seller with additional capital gains tax on the difference; and
- charge the purchaser with gifts tax and with stiff penalties if the difference between the two prices is more than 20 per cent.

It is strongly recommended that you insist that the full price is shown on the *escritura*.

## 2.7 Loans to buy a plot

It is often not necessary to pay the whole purchase price immediately. Many developers offer a range of options which usually
include a discount for immediate settlement and payment over five
or so years with interest payable at a higher rate than generally
available in the UK.

If the seller demands payment in full, a loan against property may
be obtainable from a Spanish bank, or a British bank or financial
institution. Spanish banks may grant loans up to 80 per cent, though
in practice residents are usually limited to 70 per cent and non-
residents to 50 per cent. With British banks and institutions it is
possible to obtain loans up to 100 per cent. UK branches of Spanish
banks lend up to 60 per cent repayable over 10 years. Arrangement
fees are usually about 1 per cent.

In Spain mortgage periods tend to be shorter than in the UK. The
bank will usually grant a loan for between 3 and 20 years to a
resident, and between 3 and 10 years to a non-resident. The bank's
security is by a mortgage, *hipoteca*. The usual choice of a repayment
mortgage or an endowment mortgage is offered. No guarantors are
required.

For a UK resident to obtain a loan from a Spanish bank, five
conditions must be met.

1 Permission must be obtained from the Spanish Director
General of Foreign Transactions (form TE 13).
2 The loan must be to buy a newly constructed property from a
Spanish national with Spanish residence.
3 The terms of the loan must not be more favourable than those
offered to Spanish residents.
4 Repayments must be made in 'convertible pesetas' or internal
pesetas.
5 The loan must be secured on the property by a mortgage.

The bank manager may also require a guarantee from a Spanish
resident.

There can be a problem with UK taxation on a loan to buy a
foreign property (see Section 2.18).

## 2.8 Looking after the property

A non-resident owner should have someone who lives permanently
in Spain to look after the property and pay necessary expenses, even

though this is not required under Spanish law.

The law does require a resident to file a wealth tax return on behalf of the property owner. Many British owners of Spanish properties have overlooked this fact. The Spanish authorities are now clamping down on wealth tax returns while offering a limited amnesty to those whose returns are in arrears. If you have failed to file wealth tax returns and make a voluntary disclosure of this to the authorities, you will have to pay the arrears of tax plus interest. If you make no disclosure but are caught, you will have to pay the tax, a penalty of three times the tax, and interest. Also you will experience delays in repatriating your capital and could also incur legal fees.

A Spanish bank may be willing to arrange payment of expenses, but it will not arrange maintenance of the property. Not all Spanish banks can be relied on.

It is common to instruct an agent, known as an *agente de inmuebles*, or a *gestor*. A *gestor* has no British equivalent. He handles financial and legal paperwork which relates to property. He is an expert at processing the bureaucratic paperwork endemic to Spain. He will not, however, look after the property, for which an *agente* will have to be engaged or alternative arrangements made.

## 2.9 Rates and taxes

The owner of property is liable to pay rates known as *contribuciones urbana* for town property and *contribución territorial rústica* for country property.

Local authorities also charge taxes known as *derechos y tasas sobre la propiedad inmueble*, or *tasas* for short, for various services such as sewerage and beach cleaning.

Both the rates and *tasas* are payable once or (occasionally) twice a year depending on the area. Most authorities demand payment between 15 September and 15 November. No demands are sent out, as with British rates, but fines of 20 per cent are imposed if they are not paid on time. The town hall, *Ayuntamiento*, can register a charge against the property if the rates remain unpaid.

A return for the rates is made by completing form 899 if the property is registered in your name, or form 099 if it is not. The form is obtained from tobacconists and costs 10 pesetas. It is a three-part document and must be completed in ballpoint pen or by typewriter.

The Spanish government is considering radical reforms in the rating system which could lead to some rates being doubled, particularly in the suburbs. In 1985 some town halls imposed surcharges on the rates. The Constitutional Court declared these surcharges to be illegal and thus repayable. However, they are not repaid automatically and must be claimed by the ratepayer.

Spain also has a wealth tax (Sections 3.12 to 3.14) for individuals, not for companies. This requires an annual return. The actual amounts payable will often be small – capital of £100,000 only generates a wealth tax liability of £200 a year – but the return is regarded as important as a means of reconciling an individual's income with his assets to prevent tax evasion.

Income tax is due on the notional rent of 2 per cent of the *valor catastral*. See Section 3.21.

## 2.10 New buildings

There are three types of land:

1 Rural land (*terrano rustico*)
   Such land is *not* zoned for building. It may be in urban areas, as it does mean farmland or agricultural land.
2 Urban land (*urbano*)
   Land zoned for building, subject to planning permission and building permits.
3 Urbanisable land (*terrano urbanisable*)
   This is land where you can, in principle, build but where certain additional and often expensive preliminary steps (such as the installation of roads, drains etc) have to be taken before permission to build will be granted.

If you are having a property built from scratch, the same legal procedures are generally followed as for an existing property. The same cautions that apply to having a UK property built apply in Spain, particularly the need to use a reputable lawyer.

You no longer need to have a special permit to buy development land in Spain, but you do have to complete a form TE 7, usually at the office of a *notario*.

On completion of the building work, much paperwork is produced and here it is particularly important to have professional advice.

The first document is the *Cedula de Habitabilidad* (Habitation Certificate).

This certificate is necessary to get the next two: the *Boletin de Instalaciones Eléctricas* and the *Certificado de Fin de Obra* (Certificate of

Electrical Installation and Certificate of Completion of Work). These are necessary to ensure the supply of electricity, gas bottles and the installation of a water meter. The developer will usually charge for connection.

If a dispute has arisen between the builder and the electrician, you could find the certificates withheld. This is why the contract should stipulate that the builder may not withhold the certificate for any reason.

It is possible to buy properties while they are under construction, usually at a substantial discount on the completed price. The usual cautions about the law and inspecting the property apply.

## 2.11 Utilities

Electricity and water bills must be paid promptly or supplies will be cut off without question. There is a standing charge for electricity payable every two months, even if no electricity is used.

Gas is provided in cylinders as there are no gas mains.

Telephone bills are sent out every two months by Telefonica who are quick to cut off (and slow to reconnect) telephones when the bill remains unpaid. Reconnection costs are high. See also Section 1.16.

The water supply in Spain can be erratic. There have been severe water shortages in some areas during the last few summers. Demand is continuing to rise dramatically, with more and more property being developed, and the water system is barely keeping up. Prices are rising.

Spanish water companies are mostly municipal. A resident should contact the water company by going to the water office (normally in the town hall) with his passport, habitation certificate (*Cedula de Habitabilidad*), and the number of his Spanish bank account. This is a simple procedure and the contract is straightforward. A deposit is payable, as is the cost of installing the water meter.

The bill, which is bi-monthly, is made up as follows:

1 The service fee or *cuota de servicio* – a fixed amount.
2 The consumption or *cuota de consuma* – the cost of water used.
3 The conservation fee or *cuota de conservacion* – a charge for maintaining the meter installation.
4 *IVA* (VAT) of 6 per cent on the service fee and consumption, and 15 per cent on the conservation fee.

It is advisable to pay by standing order, but check the figures against your bill.

## 2.12 Resisting sales pitches

In 1986, 700 Britons complained to the Spanish embassy in London about fraudulent property deals. Most involved fraudulent developers or sham estate agents.

It has been known for potential buyers to be pressurised into buying using the argument that there are other potential buyers and delaying may result in losing the property. Such talk should be vigorously resisted. It may just be salesman's talk aimed at closing the deal while you are still keen, but until you have consulted a Spanish lawyer you do not know for certain. It is better to lose the opportunity to buy the property than lose your money.

The British consulates in Spain (listed in Appendix 1) will recommend a suitable lawyer to you.

If you are told that the deal is off unless you sign on the spot, ask why the deal cannot stand up to scrutiny.

It has been reported that some timeshare agents employ poor people to pester tourists. There is little that can be done to resist this except completely ignoring them and complaining to the town hall. Assaulting them is an offence!

## 2.13 Importing furniture, personal goods and pets

Foreigners establishing a permanent residence in Spain are allowed to import their furniture and belongings into Spain free of all customs duties, provided that they have owned the imported items for at least six months before importation.

In practice British nationals have a disadvantage over other EC nationals. British nationals usually have to deposit a bond against import duties. The bond is reclaimed on Spanish residence. The amount of the bond can be substantial.

To import your furniture and other belongings, you need to complete four forms. These forms are often held by specialist international movers such as Arts International Movers of Hassocks, West Sussex (04446 47551).

1 An application form, *cambio de residencia*, which is available from the Spanish Consulate General. This document, which must be signed by the owner of the goods, is the form against which 'free entry' (see above) is allowed. If the furniture is for your second home, the form required is the *residencia secundaria*.
2 An itemised list in Spanish and English (signed by the owner of

the goods and submitted in duplicate) of items to be imported showing estimated values in pesetas including serial numbers and make of major electrical items. The values shown should be low second-hand prices, not insured values.

3 Photocopies of the first five pages of the applicant's passport.

4 Proof of either already possessing or having applied for a residence permit. If the permit has not yet been granted, proof of a deposit account or bank guarantee may also be required as well as a copy of the purchase or rental agreement of your property.

If importing property for a second residence in Spain, a different application form is used, one for a secondary residence, *vivienda secundaria*. The applicant also has to show the *escritura* for the first property to both Customs and the Spanish Consulate. Customs will also require either a deposit or two-year bank guarantee for 33 per cent of the value of your Spanish inventory from a Spanish-resident bank to ensure that the goods will remain in the same premises which will not be let or sublet but be reserved for his or his family's exclusive use. The guarantee is not needed if you have a *residencia*.

In the case of either a first or second residence, when permission has been granted, the items may be imported together or in batches over a period of 12 months, from the first importation.

If goods are inherited, they are imported as above, but the applicant must also submit a notarised death certificate and a notarised trustee or executor's settlement of the estate. The inherited goods may then be imported in batches at any time within two years of taking possession of the inheritance.

Wedding gifts may be imported against the usual import documents plus a notarised wedding certificate. The goods may then be imported in stages up to two months before the wedding and up to four months afterwards.

There are restrictions which ban some items from importation to Spain altogether. The restrictions largely follow UK practice and include such things as weapons (see below), illicit drugs, pornography and items made from protected species of animal.

A private car may be imported free of customs duty (33 per cent) provided it has been registered in the person's name for at least six months before taking up Spanish residence. You must also obtain a declaration before the Spanish Consulate in the UK or the British Consulate in Spain that you intend leaving the UK to live in Spain. You must also prove that VAT was paid in the UK. The car is then re-registered in Spain. It is a condition that the car is not sold or otherwise transferred within one year of the vehicle's re-registration in Spain.

Pets can generally be brought into the country freely without the need for quarantine. You need to produce two documents in respect of each pet:

- a health certificate signed by a veterinary surgeon authorised for that purpose by the Ministry of Agriculture that must be issued within the 25 days before the animal's entry to Spain; and
- a certificate issued by the Ministry of Agriculture to the effect that the animal has been kept in an area free of rabies and other animal diseases.

These documents do not have to be notarised. Remember, if your pet is returned to the UK it will spend six months in a UK quarantine.

Firearms may be imported only on presentation to the Spanish Consulate General of a valid UK firearms certificate (or valid certificate from another recognised country). A copy of the certificate must be given to the consulate for their retention. A Spanish firearms certificate will then be issued.

Importing goods for business use is subject to a different procedure. Full advice can be obtained from the Department of Trade and Industry.

### 2.14 Sending goods by post

Letters, parcels and other items of mail can generally be sent to Spain with few restrictions. Letters can be sent at the same rate as for first class mail in the UK. Postal items still need to clear the import procedure unless they have been specifically declared as exempt or the Spanish authorities are otherwise satisfied that the items are not for a commercial purpose.

Letter post may not be used for sending coins or banknotes; bearer securities; precious metals and stones (unless in an insured envelope); cotton seed; lottery tickets; narcotics; playing cards; postcards decorated with embroidery or glitter glass (unless in properly secured envelopes); printed material contrary to Spanish morality or customs; and tobacco. There are restrictions on dangerous substances.

Parcel post may not be used for sending letters; military weapons; playing cards; printed matter contrary to Spanish morals and customs; saccharin and products containing saccharin; soil and tobacco. The same restrictions apply for dangerous substances as for letter post.

There are restrictions on animal products; books and printed matter in Spanish; drugs and pharmaceutical preparations; jewellery and precious articles; plants and parts of plants; vegetables; rosaries, relics and other devotional articles; and Spanish banknotes.

In Spain, postal items are not delivered but collected from the post office by the addressee.

When a Customs declaration is necessary for a letter, this is effected by the standard 'green label' for up to £50, and the top part of the green label with form C2/CP3 for over £50. For parcel post, one non-adhesive form and despatch note must accompany each parcel. Customs declarations must show the Post Office serial number for each parcel. For all this documentation, Spanish and French are the preferred languages.

Compensation is available on request for most items. For porcelain, glassware and other exceptionally fragile articles, compensation is only payable if the damage is sustained by the UK postal service.

VAT considerations are considered in Section 3.20.

## 2.15 Timesharing

Timesharing is a particular problem in Spain, as Spanish property law does not recognise timesharing, though there is a draft law to rectify this. Timeshare agreements are governed by the law of contract in the state where the agreement is made (unless the agreement specifies another law). In practice, timesharing agreements are only as good as the timeshare company. To ensure that the contract is valid under Spanish law, it is essential to obtain the services of a Spanish lawyer, recommended by a British consulate if necessary.

Nevertheless timesharing has mushroomed in popularity in recent years. Under the system you buy the right to use the property for specified periods of each year. There is a managing agent who arranges for the property to be properly maintained and for all insurance, rates etc to be paid.

Timesharing can have many advantages over buying a property outright. The cost is less, the risk of vacant property is less, and the administration is taken care of. In many schemes your timeshare may be exchanged for a holiday in another place. The timeshares can be sold, though not always at a profit. Some timeshares bought for £5000 can now be sold for only £1000. The managing agent will often arrange a sale for you.

Unfortunately there are unscrupulous operators in the timeshare business, and potential investors are advised to check that the managing agent has legal title and operates a fair system. Timeshares usually offer a leasehold interest, either for a fixed term or in perpetuity. This is known as a 'right to use'.

There are over 30 companies which offer timeshares in Spain. The two largest companies dealing in timeshare exchanges are Resorts Condominium International and Interval International.

Timesharing can prove helpful in deciding whether to live in Spain. It allows you to try the life on a part-time basis for low cost.

## 2.16 Letting the property

There is nothing to stop you allowing friends to use your property in your absence, whether or not you charge them for doing so. The usual precautions about the people being trustworthy and responsible apply as for any letting.

If you wish to let the property to strangers for a holiday, you must first obtain a certificate registering the property as a tourist-letting entity. This is not withheld in practice. You then have to make a tax contribution of 20 per cent of your holiday rental income.

You should check the tenants' suitability (as far as is possible) and have a written agreement for the period of the tenancy. The tenancy agreement should cover:

- period of letting;
- rent payable and any deposit held;
- any extra charges for electricity, gas, telephone etc;
- any rights (usually none) to assign or sub-let; and
- responsibility to look after the property and its contents, to leave it clean and tidy, and liability for damage and repairs.

For longer lettings, it is essential to have a proper agreement drawn up by a Spanish lawyer (or a British lawyer with specialist knowledge).

Generally the owner is free to charge whatever rent he can get. There will often be a ready reference market of similar properties from which a figure can be determined. If not, a Spanish lawyer, an *agente* or a *gestor* may be able to advise. In the unlikely event that the property was built with government assistance, the government fixes the maximum rent payable.

It is important to remember that Spain has laws similar to Britain which are designed to protect people against eviction from what has become their homes. The relevant statute is the *Ley de Arrendamientos Urbanos*, the Law of Urban Lettings, which is very complicated.

Lettings for holidays or in consequence of employment are specifically excluded from the law's scope. Lettings for more than a year or for an indefinite period are included. The rule regarding indefinite periods particularly can be a trap. Any tenant who is resident in Spain enjoys this protection, even if he became resident in Spain after the tenancy began.

Such a protected tenant gains three advantages.

- The tenancy can only be terminated for certain specified reasons.
- The rent may only be increased by limited amounts. These are fixed percentages announced in the *Bolétin Oficial del Estado* and based on the increase in the cost of living.
- A fixed tenancy period may (with a few exceptions) be extended.

The landlord may evict a protected tenant by court order on the following grounds.

1 Failure to pay the rent (but if this is due to his being out of work, the court will usually give him time to pay before allowing eviction).
2 Unlawfully sub-letting the property. Sub-letting furnished property is always unlawful. A sub-letting to two or more tenants is unlawful if the landlord has not been notified of their names within 30 days. Otherwise the sub-letting is regarded as unlawful according to the terms of the tenancy agreement.
3 Sub-letting the property (lawfully) but for more than the legally authorised rent.
4 Assigning the whole property without the landlord's consent.
5 Converting the property to a shop, factory or other business use. Incidental private work such as writing, painting or private tuition does not count.
6 Causing serious damage to the property or making substantial alterations without the landlord's permission.
7 Using the property for immoral purposes.
8 Creating a danger on the premises.
9 Causing a serious nuisance or annoyance to the neighbours.

A landlord may also be able to obtain possession on the grounds that he needs the property for his own occupation or for his children's occupation. The landlord must give a year's notice and pay a sum equal to a year's rent in compensation. It is advisable to send the notice by a *notario* so that there is no dispute that the tenant received it. If the tenant leaves for any reason during the year's notice, he is entitled to a refund of a year's rent. If he stays after the year's notice, he loses his right to compensation and the landlord can apply to the court to evict him within four months.

If the tenancy is for a fixed period or periods exceeding more than one year in total, the tenant has the right to have his tenancy extended subject to certain exceptions. The main reasons for which a landlord may legally refuse an extension are:

- the landlord wants to live in the property because his family has increased making his own home overcrowded;
- the landlord has recently married and wants the property as his matrimonial home;
- the tenant is absent from the premises for more than six months a year without good reason – good reasons include employment overseas and military service;
- the tenant has more than one dwelling in the same town or village and these are more than is necessary for his and his family's needs; and
- the tenant has suitable alternative accommodation for himself and his family.

On the death of the tenant, his family enjoy the same protection. 'Family' here means wife (unless legally separated), and children, grandchildren, parents and grandparents who live with the tenant. Brothers and sisters are protected if they have lived with the tenant for two years or more before his death.

### 2.17 Living as a member of a Community of Owners

Most people who buy property in Spain will be members of a Community of Owners, a sort of tenants' co-operative. Even though the tenants may be the freehold owners of their properties, there will usually be common parts: halls, staircases, patios, swimming pools, gardens, verandas etc. The law is governed by 'The Law of Horizontal Ownership' (though it applies to high-rise flats as well!).

Each community has its own set of rules. Each member is

allocated shares according to the size of his property. The rules will determine what 'property' is for their purposes. The number of shares determines the size of his contribution to the Community and his number of votes.

The members elect from their number a chairman or *presidente* who is legally personally responsible for the Community and seeing that it obeys Spanish law. In practice the chairman often appoints an administrator. Sometimes they also appoint a secretary and a treasurer. The administrator, secretary and treasurer need not be Community members, but the chairman must be. The law, however, only requires the appointment of a chairman.

The chairman is responsible for ensuring the smooth running of the Community. This includes arranging for the repairs and maintenance of the common parts, drawing up a budget for such purposes and collecting each member's share of that budget. It is usual for annual accounts to be prepared.

Each Community has an annual general meeting for which six days' notice must be given to all members (14 days if the member lives overseas). There is no time limit for an extraordinary general meeting, provided all members are notified in time. Members may attend themselves or send a proxy. Extraordinary meetings are called by the chairman, or a member or members who hold at least 25 per cent of the shares.

A curiosity of the law is that notification of the annual meeting is made to the member's address, but notification of extraordinary meetings must be to the member. So, if a member lives overseas for most of the year, it can take longer to call an extraordinary meeting.

The meeting elects a chairman for the coming year, approves the accounts and budget, fixes each member's contribution for the forthcoming year and deals with any other matters of mutual interest. These resolutions are passed by a simple majority of votes, provided that at least 50 per cent of the voting power is represented. There is protection for aggrieved minorities who, under certain clearly defined circumstances, may apply to the courts.

One resolution often passed is that the meetings are conducted in the language of the majority present (provided an interpreter is provided for each minority language), or that all Community documents are provided in an English translation.

The meeting may also vote to change its rules, including the voting rights of its members. This must be carried unanimously. If all the members are not represented at the meeting, such a resolution may be provisionally carried by all those who are represented. A *notario* then sends details to the absent members who have one month within which to disagree. If they do not communicate dissent within the month, they are regarded as having agreed.

Each Community must keep a minute book which records attendance and resolutions of the Community. It must be written in Spanish and signed by the chairman.

If you do not pay the Community charges, your property can be sold at auction to pay the unpaid fees.


## 2.18  UK tax warning

The interest on loans to buy Spanish property does not qualify for income tax relief, either under the MIRAS scheme or otherwise.

Not only that but a UK resident who pays interest to a foreign bank must deduct income tax at the basic rate of tax from the payments, and pay the tax to the Inland Revenue. The UK/Spain tax treaty reduces this deduction to 10 per cent (the basic rate of 25 per cent less 15 per cent). Permission to deduct the lower rate must be obtained *in advance* from:

Inland Revenue
Double Taxation Rates and Inspector of Foreign Dividends
Lynwood Road
Thames Ditton
Surrey KT7 0DP; 01-398 4242

Permission will not be given retrospectively.

The tax deducted, 'withholding tax', can be reclaimed from the overseas bank subject to the contract governing the bank loan. Many foreign banks state 'all interest is payable net of all withholding taxes'. If this or a similar clause is in the contract with the foreign bank, it means that they can demand full payment from you *and claim back the withholding tax for their own benefit*. In other words you lose out both ways.

Also remember that interest payable on a bank loan to purchase an overseas property is not allowable against rental income, even though UK tax is due on the Spanish rental income if you are UK resident. Any Spanish taxes paid on the rental income may be offset against the UK tax liability.

Points to watch are:

1  If possible, borrow from a UK bank, some of which will accept foreign property as a security or will accept a guarantee from a foreign bank.

2 If you do borrow from a foreign bank, insist that the repayments are 'gross of withholding tax'.
3 Do not try to claim interest relief under MIRAS or otherwise.
4 Remember to complete your Spanish wealth tax return.

If you have a Spanish *residencia* you can claim a tax allowance of 17 per cent of the capital cost of buying a new house or 15 per cent of the cost of a second-hand property. Non-residents cannot make this claim.

### 2.19 Example of costs

As an example of the total costs of a new property:

| On purchase | Section reference | Pesetas | |
|---|---|---|---|
| Purchase price | | | 9,000,000 |
| 6% IVA | 2.6 | 540,000 | |
| *Plus Valía* | 2.6 | 40,000 | |
| *Notary fee* | 2.6 | 70,000 | |
| *Registration fee* | 2.6 | 30,000 | |
| Electricity contract | 2.10 | 75,000 | |
| Water contract | 2.10 | 25,000 | |
| Legal fees | 2.1 | 135,000 | 915,000 |
| | | | 9,915,000 |

The annual running costs for such a property might be:

| Annual costs | Section reference | Pesetas |
|---|---|---|
| Local rates | 2.9 | 54,000 |
| Local charges | 2.9 | 5,000 |
| Community fee | 1.17 | 40,000 |
| Electricity | 2.11 | 84,000 |
| Water | 2.11 | 10,000 |
| Insurance | | 25,000 |
| Wealth tax | 3.13 | 19,000 |
| Income tax | 3.4 | 20,000 |
| Tax consultants | | 15,000 |
| | | 272,000 |

Note that repairs and maintenance have not been included. This example has been reproduced from the magazine *Spain Today*, which is an excellent publication available free to all members of the Institute of Foreign Property Owners (address in Appendix 1).

## 2.20 Other Matters

On buying a property in Spain you should prepare a Spanish will (and perhaps revise your British one). The property needs to be insured. You have to appoint a local fiscal representative, pay your local rates, make a wealth tax return, if relevant, pay car tax and insurance if you have a car, and pay your utility bills. All these points are discussed elsewhere in the book.

Even if you have purchased your property as a second home, you are liable to tax – see Section 3.21.

## 2.21 Advantages and disadvantages of different types of property

This section is based on notes prepared by John Howell & Company, solicitors who have offices in Spain and Sheffield (see Appendix 5).

|  | Advantages | Disadvantages |
|---|---|---|
| Old farmhouses | Character; good capital growth as limited supply; few planning problems | Sometimes built badly; alterations can be complex; often no utilities; repair costs high |
| Purpose-built detached villas | Easy to resell; good privacy; usually well built | Expensive; usually large gardens; often on mountain sides and can have foundation problems; security poor |
| Linked villas (terraced) | Easy to resell; usually well built | Noisy; Community of Owners to deal with; lack of privacy |

| | | |
|---|---|---|
| Duplex | Cheap | As for linked villas, but more so; often used as holiday lets – noisy |
| Apartments | Even cheaper; communal; good security; low running costs | As for linked villas, but more so; noisy neighbours; Community fees can be high; often utilities are supplied to a community which sub-supplies to you – if they don't pay you get cut off. |

# Chapter 3

# Taxation of Individuals in Spain

## 3.1 Introduction

It should be understood from the outset that liability to Spanish tax is determined solely by *de facto* residence. The liability is not in any way affected by having or not having a work permit or residence permit. Many expatriates in Spain wrongly believe that living on a 90-day tourist visa protects them from Spanish tax.

Spain is not a tax haven. Its rates of income tax go up to 56 per cent in 1989 and capital gains are taxed as income (see Section 3.6). Using 1989 rates, a married person earning £60,000 will pay £14,500 in the UK but £28,500 in Spain.

In Spain taxes are levied at two levels: national taxes are levied by the government (or autonomous province) and local taxes by the municipal authorities.

The government taxes are administered by the Ministry of Economy and Taxation, *Ministerio de Económia y Hacienda* (or its equivalent in the provinces). The ministry is usually simply referred to as the *Hacienda*. The government taxes comprise:

- corporate income tax, *impuesto sobre sociedades*;
- personal income tax, *impuesto sobre la renta de las personas fisicas*;
- value added tax, *impuesto sobre el valor añadido (IVA)*;
- wealth tax; and
- inheritance and gift tax, *impuesto sobre sucesiones y donaciones*.

The local taxes are:

- property taxes, *contribucíon urbana*;
- municipal gains tax, *plus valía*; and
- various licence fees.

Unlike the UK, partnerships pay the corporate income tax.

Investment companies controlled by a few members are not taxed corporately. The members are taxed individually on their share of the profits.

The *Hacienda* has its administrative headquarters in Madrid and sub-assessment and tax collection centres in major towns. Provinces have tax headquarters in their principal cities.

Personal income tax is levied on individuals.

The Spanish tax year is the same as the calendar year.

The self-assessment system is used.

A useful provision of the Spanish tax system is that written questions may be addressed to the Ministry for a written answer (usually given in two or three months) regarding the tax implications of a specific transaction. The answer is binding on the tax authorities on the transaction in question.

The current tax laws were formulated in 1978 and are amended annually in a Budget. There are also ministerial orders.

Up to 1986 the Spanish tax collection authorities were very inefficient. When VAT was introduced on 1 January 1986, this tax, which was simple to collect (and therefore hard to avoid), showed up many new taxpayers (1.3 million to be precise), with the result that tax revenues from personal income tax increased by 36 per cent, from corporate income tax by 34 per cent and from wealth tax by 44 per cent. The income from VAT itself was four times the Spanish government estimate!

The Spanish tax man is paid a bonus based on the amount of tax collected. The tax authorities use computers extensively. They have ten small aircraft equipped with the most up-to-date cameras which are used to photograph each dwelling, apartment block and farm (and so far they have found over 8 million properties not on the tax register). Despite all this, tax evasion in Spain is rife.

## 3.2 Residence

Liability to pay Spanish income tax depends on residence under laws similar to those which apply in Britain. For individuals, residence is *de facto* residence, regardless of whether the person has a residence permit or work permit.

An individual is resident if physically present in Spain for at least 183 days in the year. A husband and wife used to be both regarded as Spanish residents if either of them met the residence requirement. This has now been altered by a Constitutional Court ruling in January 1989 which states that the 'family unit' concept is wrong, and that husband and wife must be taxed separately. An individual who is regarded as Spanish-resident pays tax on his worldwide income. An individual who is regarded as not a Spanish resident only pays Spanish income tax on his income which arises within Spain.

A non-resident personal income tax payer must appoint an agent in Spain.

A company is regarded as resident in Spain if:

- its registered office is in Spain;
- it was incorporated in Spain; or
- its effective centre of management is in Spain.

Resident companies pay corporate income tax on their worldwide profits. Non-resident companies pay corporate income tax on income and capital gains from Spanish sources only.

### 3.3  Tax returns

Everyone who is Spanish resident must make a tax return if his income exceeds 865,000 pesetas from earned income or 206,000 pesetas of unearned income. He must disclose all his income regardless of the country of origin. Although the income limits of 865,000 and 206,000 pesetas apply to foreigners, it is better to make a declaration even though you are under the limit as you need to present the return to renew your residence permit.

Anyone who is not resident in Spain is only liable to pay tax if his income exceeds 840,000 pesetas.

Husband and wife are now taxed as two separate persons.

Tax returns are obtained, believe it or not, from tobacconists or the tax office. To add insult to injury, you have to pay for a blank tax return form.

There are two types of form; the *declaración simplificada* (form D-101) and the *declaración ordinaria* (form D-100). The former is used if your income is less than 1.59 million pesetas; it is a simple document comprising just two pages. The latter is used if your income is higher, and runs to 13 pages. You can obtain the forms from a tobacconist shop (*tabacaleria*) but you should consider using a Spanish professional adviser (who can always obtain the forms).

Tax returns must be filed between 1 May and 20 June in the year after the tax year. In 1989 these dates were delayed. If a repayment of tax is due, the latter date is deferred to 30 June. The taxpayer either pays the whole amount of tax with his return, or pays 60 per cent of the tax with the return, and the balance by 5 November following.

The tax return and payments are made:

- at the local tax office;

- at any bank or savings bank (in which case the payment must be by bank transfer); or
- by post (for which a Bank of Spain draft is required).

A non-resident must appoint a tax representative in Spain who is jointly responsible for the non-resident's payment of all taxes, including capital gains tax on the sale of any property in Spain. The form to be used is form 210, and you will not find it at the *tabacaleria*, but your tax representative should have a supply. This form has to be submitted to the *Hacienda* by January each year for the previous tax year.

In 1989 all the time limits were postponed to September when the Spanish Constitutional Court found that the 'family form' was illegal, as both husband and wife should not be forced to make a joint declaration. In future, separate forms will be produced. You should not submit a joint declaration as this may increase your tax liability.

### 3.4 Scope of personal income tax

Taxable income includes all wages, salaries, benefits in kind, rents, business profits, royalties etc. Unlike the UK system, capital gains are also included in income (see Section 3.6) although they form a separate pool of income for tax purposes. All income is aggregated; there is no equivalent to the UK system of schedules.

Added to this income is the notional rental value of any property owned. This is fixed at 2 per cent of the *valor catastral*, the rateable value of the property. The *valor catastral* is shown in box 5b in the receipt for local rates (*contribución urbana*) and is set by the *Hacienda*. These values have been ridiculously low, but are now being actively revised to about 70 per cent of the real value.

The *valor catastral* affects:

- the amount of rates you pay;
- the amount of income tax due as the rentable value of your house is treated as income;
- your wealth tax return;
- any gift or inheritance tax due.

The *Hacienda* intend to revise the values of 14 million properties in 1989 and 1990.

A few categories of income are tax-free. These include termination payments (to certain limits), lottery prizes, industrial injury awards and certain awards for personal achievement (as decided by the *Hacienda*).

Disbursements are not taxable. However, payments in excess of approved rates for travel and subsistence are taxed. Profits on share dealings and maturation of insurance policies are also included as income (see Section 3.6).

### 3.5 Deductions from personal income tax

You may deduct from your tax the following items which are also tax-deductible in the UK:

- mortgage interest;
- working expenses; and
- approved amount of travel and subsistence payments.

You may also deduct these items which are not usually tax-deductible in the UK:

- medical expenses;
- house repairs; and
- a percentage of buying a house.

Deductions for administration and custody of investment certificates are allowed. Interest is allowed on borrowed capital up to a limit of 800,000 pesetas per person (ie 1.6 million for husband and wife) if you are a Spanish resident.

You are allowed to deduct interest on capital borrowed for investment in owner-occupied property and on sums invested in obtaining rental income. The interest deduction is limited to 800,000 pesetas. You can also write off 15 per cent of the cost of the property in the year of purchase, subject to certain limits.

Also deductible are contributions to mutual societies, social security payments, sundry charitable donations and a general deduction of 2 per cent from earnings for 'expenses difficult to justify'.

There are personal allowances determined similar to those in the UK, and additional allowances for dependent children and elderly relatives. However, unlike the UK system, these are deducted from the tax payable not the taxable income (see Section 3.7).

### 3.6 Capital gains

Capital gains are included with other income for personal income tax. This section deals with how such gains are calculated.

A form of roll-over relief is granted for the sale of the taxpayer's permanent home. The property must be the principal and habitual residence of the taxpayer. For such disposals, gains up to 30,900,000 pesetas are exempt provided the proceeds are used to buy another principal home within two years. If the proceeds are not fully invested in a new home, or if the proceeds exceed the limit, the relief is restricted proportionately. This relief is not available on second homes. The tax must first be paid, and will be refunded when the next permanent home is purchased. You can only obtain the relief if you purchase the next home *after* the sale of the first, not before.

The amount of the capital gain is calculated by deducting the proceeds from the uplifted cost. The uplifted cost is determined by multiplying the original cost by a coefficient which reflects the rate of inflation. The coefficients relate to years (rather than to months as in the UK).

For 1988 and 1989 the coefficients are:

| Year of acquisition | 1989 Coefficient | 1988 Coefficient |
| --- | --- | --- |
| before 1979 | 2.333 | 2.272 |
| 1979 | 2.050 | 1.997 |
| 1980 | 1.809 | 1.763 |
| 1981 | 1.610 | 1.570 |
| 1982 | 1.438 | 1.430 |
| 1983 | 1.308 | 1.277 |
| 1984 | 1.201 | 1.173 |
| 1985 | 1.129 | 1.103 |
| 1986 | 1.062 | 1.038 |
| 1987 | 1.023 | 1.000 |
| 1988 | 1.000 | – |

This inflation-adjusted gain is then divided by the number of years of ownership of the asset. This amount is taxed as income subject to the progressive rates of income tax. The balance is taxed at the average effective rate of personal income tax on the taxpayer's income for the year.

For assets purchased before 31 December 1978, the value at that date is used. This is the same figure as for wealth tax. For an asset received as a gift or inheritance, the figure used should be that given on the inheritance and gift tax return. For insurance policies, the cost is the sum of premiums paid. For non-residents the rate is 35 per cent.

**Table 1**   *Income tax rates for 1989*

| A<br>From pesetas | B<br>To pesetas | Cumulative tax<br>due on Column A | % on amounts in<br>excess of Column A |
|---|---|---|---|
| nil | 618,000 | nil | nil |
| 618,000 | 1,030,000 | nil | 25 |
| 1,030,000 | 1,545,000 | 103,000 | 26 |
| 1,545,000 | 2,060,000 | 236,900 | 27 |
| 2,060,000 | 2,575,000 | 375,950 | 28 |
| 2,575,000 | 3,090,000 | 520,150 | 30 |
| 3,090,000 | 3,605,000 | 674,650 | 32 |
| 3,605,000 | 4,120,000 | 839,450 | 34 |
| 4,120,000 | 4,635,000 | 1,014,550 | 36 |
| 4,635,000 | 5,150,000 | 1,199,950 | 38.5 |
| 5,150,000 | 5,665,000 | 1,398,225 | 41 |
| 5,665,000 | 6,180,000 | 1,609,375 | 43.5 |
| 6,180,000 | 6,695,000 | 1,833,400 | 46 |
| 6,695,000 | 7,210,000 | 2,070,300 | 48.5 |
| 7,210,000 | 7,725,000 | 2,320,075 | 51 |
| 7,725,000 | 8,240,000 | 2,582,725 | 53.5 |
| 8,240,000 | and over | 2,858,250 | 56 |

For a Spanish resident the combined liability to income tax and wealth tax cannot exceed 70 per cent of total taxable income.

## 3.7  Personal income tax: rates

The rates of tax payable by Spanish residents for 1989 (assessed in 1990) are subject to 17 tax bands. The first 618,000 pesetas are tax free, thereafter tax rises (not uniformly) to 56 per cent on incomes over 8,240,000 pesetas (see Table 1).

The taxpayer is entitled to a personal allowance of 23,900 pesatas if a married couple. This is increased by 18,100 pesetas for every child under 25 living with parents. There are additions for the handicapped and elderly. These allowances are deducted from the tax bill itself, not from the taxable income as in the UK.

So a single taxpayer pays no tax if his income does not exceed 618,000 pesetas and a married man pays no tax on earnings to 713,600 pesetas ([23,900 × 4] + 618,000).

Further explanation of these allowances and other tax credits is given in Section 3.8.

From 1988, payments into a pension plan will qualify for tax relief, so that 15 per cent of the amount paid is deducted from taxable income.

## 3.8 Tax credits

The taxpayer is entitled to make various tax credits, which sums are deducted from his tax, not taxable income.

There are allowances for marriage (currently 23,900 pesetas), for each unmarried child under 25 supported by the taxpayer (currently 18,100 pesetas), for each parent (or remoter ancestor) living with the taxpayer who is either over 70 or earns less than 618,000 pesetas, and for each severely handicapped member of the family.

The main wage-earner in a family is entitled to an employment income credit of 29,200 pesetas (for 1989). A second wage-earner is entitled to a credit of 1 per cent of earnings to a maximum of 10,500 pesetas. Other wage-earners are not entitled to this credit. If there is more than one earner a further variable deduction may be taken to a maximum of 412,000 pesetas.

There is a tax credit for personal expenses equal to 15 per cent of duly substantiated expenses paid because of illness, accident or disability of the taxpayer, or because of hospitalisation or medical treatment in connection with the birth of the taxpayer's child. Amounts paid in medical insurance are tax deductible.

To encourage life insurance, 15 per cent of the premiums paid for life and/or disability insurance are deductible (with restrictions for insurance policies of less than 10 years' duration). The policy's beneficiary must be the taxpayer, a member of his family unit, spouse, ancestor or descendant.

To encourage property ownership, 17 per cent of the cost of any new dwelling is tax deductible, whatever its use. A deduction of 15 per cent is given for second-hand properties. Thus property acquired for letting comes within this scope. Capital gains on the sale of the property are exempt up to 30,900,000 pesetas if rolled over into a new property.

There are similar concessions for the purchase of historic buildings and of items of cultural interest.

For qualifying securities, 10 per cent of the purchase price paid for shares bought on the Spanish stock exchange may be credited. This is subject to their not being sold for three years from the date of purchase.

For dividends, 10 per cent of the amount received may be credited against the shareholder's personal income tax liability. As the company will already have paid corporate income tax, this recent development is moving towards the system used in the UK.

Items of cultural interest donated to the state (including public bodies and institutions) qualify for 20 per cent tax relief.

The maximum amount of credit that may be granted for investment, property, historic buildings and cultural assets, qualifying securities, dividends, and gifts of cultural items is restricted to 30 per cent of the annual taxable base of the taxpayer or his family unit.


### 3.9 Personal income tax: non-residents

For 1989 (assessed in 1990) non-resident individuals are taxed on all income earned in Spain, subject to any relief granted in a double taxation treaty at a flat rate of 20 per cent for income and 35 per cent for capital gains.

Gross income (including dividends, profits, royalties and interest receivable) is taxed at 20 per cent. Copyright royalties on films are taxed at 10 per cent. Capital gains are taxed at 35 per cent.

Non-residents are not entitled to any personal allowances or tax credits unless they have a permanent address in Spain. They are then allowed to credit amounts invested in qualifying securities.

Non-residents do not benefit from the rules which limit the total tax liability to a fixed percentage.


### 3.10 Personal income tax: administration of the tax in practice

A tax return must be made by the taxpayer on a form which he buys from a tobacconist. Tax returns are not sent out automatically by the tax office, *Hacienda*. Advice is usually sought from a tax expert, *assesor fiscal*.

The returns for the last five years are liable to audit. The inspection department of the *Hacienda* compiles an annual audit list of taxpayers falling within certain criteria. If your name is chosen you must present yourself and your tax papers to the local tax office. The five-year limit means that where false tax returns are made, the *Hacienda* cannot go back more than five years. In Spain, if you failed entirely to make a return, the five-year period would begin on the last day of the legal period to declare. In the case of inheritance tax, if the government has not settled the estate within five years of the day of the death, the tax cannot be collected and the inheritors keep all the money!

A list of all local persons filing tax returns is displayed in the town hall for 30 days.

Late payment of tax gives rise to an interest charge. For simple breaches of the tax law a fine of between 1000 and 1 million pesetas may be levied for each offence. For serious breaches of the law (known as 'economic prejudice') the fine may be three times the tax evaded.

## 3.11 Corporate income tax

Corporate income tax is the Spanish equivalent of the UK's corporation tax. It is paid by all corporate bodies, which in Spain includes partnerships.

For certain types of company, the profits are subject to personal income tax in the hands of the corporate body's members. This is known as 'fiscal transparency'. It is obligatory for non-quoted investment companies, companies formed to carry on professional activities, and for asset-holding companies where either:

- more than 50 per cent of the assets are held directly or indirectly by a family group for up to 183 days of the tax year; or
- more than 50 per cent of the assets are held by ten individuals or less.

There is a single rate of 35 per cent corporate income tax. The charge to tax arises on a taxable event, *hecho imponible*. This includes the realisation of profits, capital gains and other income arising from commercial activities or exploitation of assets.

Navarra and the Basque country have their own corporate income tax systems.

The amount assessable to corporate income tax is determined by specific rules which do not always follow the country's accounting practices. The most important differences concern instalment sales and foreign currency leasing.

The deductible and non-deductible items are similar to those in the UK. An exception is that instead of capital allowances, depreciation is allowed at rates published by the tax authorities. There are similar rates published to determine the allowability of bad or doubtful debts and instalment credits.

A company must file a tax return within 25 days of its annual general meeting, which must be held within six months of its year-end. A payment on account has to be made each October. The amount is 30 per cent of the tax paid in the previous year *regardless of the current year's results.*

### 3.12 Wealth tax: outline

In addition to income tax, there is a wealth tax that was introduced in 1978.

Individuals resident in Spain pay wealth tax on all assets owned anywhere in the world and are entitled to reliefs. Non-resident individuals are taxed on their Spanish assets only but do not qualify for any reliefs.

The tax is charged on the individual's net wealth as at 31 December. Taxable assets comprise all property, investments, personal chattels and cash deposits. For property, the tax is charged on the *valor catastral* (official value), which is usually much less than the property's market value.

From this sum are deducted all debts, charges, and other personal obligations (including unpaid tax).

A further effective tax on wealth arises from the new inheritance and gift tax (Section 3.15) under which the rate of tax payable increases according to the donee's wealth and the relationship between the donor and donee.

A Spanish resident does not have to make a wealth tax return if no income tax return is needed and the assets are less than 4 million pesetas.

The wealth tax return (form D-714) must be filed between 1 May and 20 June for the previous tax year.

### 3.13 Wealth tax: rates

The rates of wealth tax are:

| From ptas | To ptas | Rate % | Tax on band ptas | Cumulative total ptas |
|---|---|---|---|---|
| 0 | 25m | 0.2 | 50,000 | 50,000 |
| 25m | 50m | 0.3 | 75,000 | 125,000 |
| 50m | 100m | 0.45 | 225,000 | 350,000 |
| 100m | 250m | 0.65 | 975,000 | 1,325,000 |
| 250m | 500m | 0.85 | 2,125,000 | 3,450,000 |
| 500m | 1000m | 1.10 | 5,500,000 | 8,950,000 |
| 1000m | 1500m | 1.35 | 6,750,000 | 15,700,000 |
| 1500m | 2500m | 1.70 | 8,500,000 | 24,200,000 |
| 2500m | no limit | 2.00 | | |

The rates have not increased since the tax was introduced in 1978 as a temporary measure. There are as yet unrealised plans to reform this tax as part of a wider tax reform.

## 3.14 Wealth tax: reliefs

Spanish-resident taxpayers only are entitled to these reliefs given against their figures of taxable wealth:

| | |
|---|---|
| single person | 9m pesetas |
| married couple | 18m pesetas |
| child | 1.5m pesetas |
| invalid/handicapped child | 1.5m pesetas |

The relief for a child is given if the child is under 25 and eligible for the personal income tax allowance.

## 3.15 Inheritance and gift tax: introduction

This tax, *impuesto sobre sucesiones y donaciones*, is restructured from 1 January 1988. The new rules are given here.

The tax is payable by:

- Spanish-resident donees and inheritors on worldwide assets; and
- non-resident donees and inheritors on assets situated in Spain.

Note that this tax differs from UK inheritance tax in that it is paid by the donee, and lifetime gifts are assessable.

The tax is only paid by individuals. Corporate bodies are liable to pay corporate income tax on the amount which is assessed as a capital gain.

Life insurance policies form part of the inheritor's taxable base whenever the life insurance policy is subscribed by the deceased.

The tax return must be filed within six months of the transfer, or else a 5 per cent surcharge may be payable.

## 3.16 Inheritance and gift tax: computation

The amount of tax payable depends on three factors:

- the relationship between the donor and donee, or deceased and inheritor;

- the amount of the gift or inheritance; and
- the existing wealth of the donee or inheritor when the gift or inheritance is received.

The relationship is determined by categorising donees and inheritors into four groups thus:

| | |
|---|---|
| Group I | children and grandchildren under 21 |
| Group II | children and grandchildren 21 or over |
| | spouses, parents and grandparents |
| Group III | brothers and sisters |
| | uncles and aunts |
| | nephews and nieces |
| | parents-in-law |
| | sons- and daughters-in-law |
| Group IV | anyone not falling in Groups I, II or III |

The amount of the gift or inheritance is known as the taxable base. A deduction is made from this taxable base according to the relationship thus:

| | |
|---|---|
| Group I | 2,060,000 pesetas, plus 515,000 pesetas for each year below 21 to a maximum of 4m pesetas |
| Group II | 2,060,000 pesetas |
| Group III | 1,030,000 pesetas |
| Group IV | no deduction |

The rate of tax varies from 7.65 to 81.6 per cent depending on three factors:

- the relationship according to the groups given above;
- the donee's net wealth before receiving the gift or inheritance; and
- the amount of the gift.

These coefficients for donee's net wealth are:

| Net wealth | Groups I & II | Group III | Group IV |
|---|---|---|---|
| 0–51.5m | 1.00 | 1.5882 | 2.0 |
| 51.5m–257.5m | 1.05 | 1.6676 | 2.1 |
| 257.5m–515m | 1.10 | 1.7471 | 2.2 |
| over 515m | 1.20 | 1.9059 | 2.4 |

## 3.17 Double taxation

Spain has tax treaties with Austria, Belgium, Brazil, Canada, Denmark, Finland, France, Germany (Federal Republic), Italy, Japan, the Netherlands, Norway, Portugal, Romania, Sweden, Switzerland, the USA (since March 1989) and Britain. Inheritance tax is not covered by these treaties.

Other treaties are being negotiated.

Treaties on income from air and sea navigation have been entered into with the USA, Mexico and most other Latin-American countries, Cuba, Gabon, Ivory Coast, Jordan, Kuwait, Lebanon, Liberia, Nigeria, South Africa, Tunisia and Zaire.

Most of these treaties closely follow the OECD model.

The UK/Spain treaty was established by a convention of 21 October 1975 which came into force on 25 November 1976. It runs to 31 articles. In the UK the treaty was effected by a statutory instrument: SI 1976 No 1919.

The treaty covers income tax, corporation tax and capital gains tax in the UK, and personal income tax, corporate income tax, certain prepayments which represent tax on land, capital, business and industrial activities, Saharan tax, surface royalties, and local taxes on income and capital.

The principal withholding tax rates for UK residents are:

dividends: 10 per cent, but 15 per cent if the recipient is a company with at least a 10 per cent holding in the paying company;
interest: 12 per cent; and
royalties: 10 per cent, but 8 per cent for film royalties.

Where there is no tax treaty, a credit is available under Spanish national law which gives *resident* taxpayers relief from foreign taxes similar to a Spanish tax. The amount of credit given is usually limited on a per country basis to the amount of Spanish corporate or personal income tax applicable to the income from the country concerned.

## 3.18 Value added tax: introduction

Value added tax, *impuesto sobre el valor añadido* or IVA, was introduced on 1 January 1986 when Spain joined the EC. It replaced the previous sales and luxury tax.

IVA operates in all Spanish territory except the Canary Islands, Ceuta and Melilla. In these areas the old sales and luxury tax is still applied.

The tax is charged on:

- all goods and services which arise in Spain; and
- all imports to Spain

unless specifically exempted.

Many IVA rules are similar to the UK rules for VAT, as both taxes come within the aegis of EC regulations.

### 3.19 Value added tax: scope

The following items are exempt:

health care (except for some private institutions);
doctors' and dentists' services;
social security services;
education;
sports and cultural activities;
state lotteries;
financial operations;
insurance;
second-hand dwellings;
rental on dwellings;
exports.

There are three rates of tax:

6 per cent (reduced rate): books, newspapers, magazines, houses, medicines, food, drink (other than alcoholic), medical sanitary items, land transport and non-luxury hotels;

12 per cent (standard rate): most items; and

33 per cent (increased rate): non-commercial vehicles, car hire for more than one month, pleasure boats (more than 9 metres in length), private aircraft, furs, jewellery, and X-films.

Spain does not have any zero-rated items.

### 3.20 Value added tax: operation

Returns are made quarterly or monthly, depending on the size of the turnover. Input tax is deducted from output tax and the balance remitted to the authorities. When the input tax exceeds the output tax, the balance is carried forward to the next period and, if necessary, periodically refunded by the authorities.

Among items for which input tax may not be deducted are business gifts, most forms of entertainment, and fuel used by employees.

There is a special procedure for recovering input tax paid in one EC country from output tax paid in another.

The tax is generally operated under the 'ordinary system' or 'simplified system'. There are special schemes for:

professional individuals;
agricultural activities;
second-hand dealers;
art and antique dealers;
retailers; and
travel agencies.

Goods on which VAT has been paid in one EC state may not be offset against a further supply in another, but a refund of output tax is claimed from the EC state on written application.

The UK retail export scheme applies to Spain from 1 January 1986. This scheme allows VAT on goods costing up to £207 (including VAT) to be sold through a retail outlet for personal export free of VAT if the necessary paperwork is completed. This is form VAT 407, which must be authenticated by the Spanish authorities on arrival there. Details of the retail export scheme are given in VAT Notice 704.

Small non-commercial consignments of goods with a value of up to £71 are exempt from VAT. The previous limits were £58 from 1 July 1986, and £40 from 15 August 1980.

### 3.21 Taxation on your second home in Spain

Merely owning a home in Spain means that you are liable to pay various Spanish taxes, and you must appoint a legal tax representative in Spain.

*Income tax.* Even if you do not let the property, you are liable for income tax on the notional rent of 2 per cent of the *valor catastral* (see Section 3.4). The tax rate is 20 per cent without any deductions. If you let the property, for those months rented the notional rent is substituted with the actual rent. Spanish income tax of 20 per cent is also due on the rental income (regardless of where paid).

*Wealth tax.* This is payable at a minimum of 0.2 per cent – see Section 3.12.

*Inheritance and gift tax.* This is due if you die, or give part or all of the home away, even though you are non-resident – see Section 3.15.

*Local rates.* See Section 2.9.

*Capital gains tax.* Thirty-five per cent in Spain (and a possible further 5 per cent in the UK to meet the higher rate of 40 per cent) roll-over relief into a new house is *not* available on second homes.

*Interest on loans.* Not tax deductible.


### 3.22 Número de identificación

There are two kinds of identity number in Spain. They have almost identical names but they are different.

1 *NIE (Número de identificación de extranjeros).* This is the identity number issued by the police to foreigners which you will need for any work permit, *permanencia, residencia* or travel document. To obtain one you should take your passport to the local police station, or supply the police with photocopies verified by the Spanish General Consulate. The *residencia* already has the NIE shown on it.

2 *NIF (Numero de identificación fiscal).* This is your tax reference number issued by the local *Hacienda* where you start a business or profession.

# Chapter 4

# Spanish Immigration and Residence Laws

## 4.1 Introduction

Spain makes few distinctions between foreigners and Spanish nationals (Section 4.5).

It does, however, make a sharp distinction between tourists and residents. Each category has its own advantages and disadvantages. There are no formalities, other than a current British passport, for a tourist. A resident needs a residence permit which has more formalities, though they are not particularly onerous.

A tourist is normally limited to a 90-day stay, though this can usually be extended for two further 90-day periods by following the formalities of obtaining a *permanencia*.

The law was considerably tightened up in 1986; in particular the practice of being a 'permanent tourist' was outlawed. Staying in Spain without a residence permit is an offence rendering the offender liable to deportation. It also denies the person certain benefits available to the resident.

Being a resident in no way affects your liability for Spanish income tax, which is assessed on *de facto* residence. Nor does it affect your rights to drive a car (Section 4.6).

This is an area where there is plenty of bad advice, and there are still many residents who would rather stay in Portugal or France every 90 days than become a resident. The consequences of getting it wrong can be disastrous, so the relevant procedures must be strictly followed.

The town halls and immigration authorities are clamping down on abuses of residence laws. They have invested in computer equipment, and take a hard line when they catch offenders. Typically, offenders are first warned to get their papers in order. If this fails they are required to leave the country and will not be allowed to return for three years.

## 4.2  British tourists

Spanish law grants generous concessions to British (and most other countries') tourists. Many of these concessions are not available to Spanish nationals or foreign residents.

You are a tourist if your stay in Spain is for no more than 90 days. You may bring your belongings and money and car into Spain without official permission; you only need a full British passport. You may bring in your car, needing only a Green Card issued by an insurance company showing at least third party liability, and a copy of the insurance certificate.

A tourist may open non-resident bank accounts and foreign currency accounts at banks.

If a tourist wishes to stay beyond 90 days, he must go to a police station which has a special department for foreigners, to apply for a *permanencia* to stay for another 90 days. There is usually no problem in obtaining an extension. You should apply to the police station about two weeks before the previous 90-day period ends. You must take with you your passport, three small photographs and confirmation from your Spanish bank that you have more than 250,000 pesetas in your account or that you have a regular pension.

Having a 90-day visa, or a *permanencia*, has absolutely no effect on your tax residence. Whether or not you have a tourist visa you will become a Spanish tax resident if you are in Spain for more than 183 days per calendar year.

You can have two *permanencias* a year, though some police stations will only grant one.

## 4.3  Residence permits

If you wish to stay in Spain for more than 90 days in a year, you must apply for a residence permit.

It is illegal to live in Spain as a permanent tourist. Before 1986 many people got away with being permanent tourists. All they did was cross the border to France or Portugal (Gibraltar didn't count) every 90 days and have their passports stamped to that effect. They did not even stay overnight in the country.

Since 1986 the position has changed, and you may now only stay in Spain for more than 90 days if you:

are a Spanish resident already;
have obtained a *permanencia*, or
have a residence permit.

To obtain a residence permit, you first need an entry visa from the Spanish consulate in the UK. The entry visa can be obtained from any Spanish embassy or consulate anywhere in the world, though in practice many refuse to issue them to people who are not nationals of the country in which they are situated. An application for an entry visa can be processed immediately at a Spanish consulate. It is recommended that you apply about five or six days before you depart, as the 90-day period starts from when the visa is granted.

You must have a full five- or ten-year British passport to enable you to obtain one from the Spanish embassy in London.

To obtain your *residencia* for the first time you must have:

- a current passport with a visa;
- a certificate from the local British consulate that you are registered there (one certificate is enough for a married couple);
- a certificate stating that you have no criminal record – the consulate will usually give you this;
- evidence of means, eg copy of your bank statement or proof of regular income;
- four passport photos;
- a certificate of good conduct from the Spanish Ministry of Justice. You can obtain the official form from your local tobacconist shop (*Certificado de antecendentes penales*) – complete it and send it to Madrid;
- evidence that you have private health insurance in Spain;
- proof of accommodation, eg copy of the *escritura* or rental contract; and
- the tax stamps (*papel de estado*), costing about 500 pesetas.

You can employ a *gestor* (lawyer) to deal with these forms or apply yourself to the *Guardia Civil* to obtain a certificate which you then take to the *Commissaria de Policia*. The application for the *residencia* must be made 45 days before the visa expires. The first *residencia* is usually now issued for two years, with a second one for five years. To renew it, you must show your income tax return.

A residence permit may be surrendered at any time to the police. You then revert to tourist status, which in practice means leaving the country within 90 days. Surrendering a permit does not prejudice your re-applying for a residence permit, nor does it restrict your returning as a tourist. A husband and wife do not have to apply jointly, and it is possible for only one spouse to have the permit.

## 4.4 Advantages of having a residence permit

If you have a residence permit, you may:

- import most chattels free of duties and taxes;
- purchase sterling for UK holidays and other purposes;
- obtain a bank loan; or
- apply for a work permit.

If you have a British retirement pension, you can also join the Spanish National Health Service.

## 4.5 Law of foreigners

Spain's law of foreigners, *ley orgánica sobre Derechos y Libertades de los Extranjeros en España*, was promulgated on 1 July 1985 and amended by a judgment of the Constitutional Court on 7 July 1987.

A foreigner is defined as someone who does not have Spanish nationality. Spain generally gives foreigners the same rights as Spanish nationals. The rights are the same for all foreigners; there are no restrictions on any particular country's nationals for lack of reciprocity or other reason.

Foreigners' rights are defined in Title 1 of the Spanish constitution and contains the following guarantees:

1 Foreigners enjoy equality of rights with Spaniards, except that they cannot vote in national elections or hold public office. They may be able to vote in municipal elections.
2 Extradition will only be granted to another country under a treaty or the operation of Spanish law. (In practice the UK has concluded a more effective extradition treaty with Spain, parts of which had previously been notorious as a haven for fugitives from British justice.)
3 Stateless persons and refugees are welcomed in accordance with the laws regarding asylum.

The law specifically allows foreigners to:

- teach or engage in scientific or professional investigation as permitted by Spanish law;
- enjoy the right of lawful free assembly (which under the Court Order cannot be made subject to official permission); and
- join trade unions.

The Constitutional Court judgment also allows administrative decisions relating to foreigners to be suspended, but bars the state's prerogative to suspend the right of free assocation.

Foreigners must obey Spanish laws (except when applicable only to nationals); are entitled to free education (see Section 1.9); and may institute their own teaching establishments. Foreigners may enter Spain freely unless specifically banned, but must enter through a recognised port, airport or frontier post unless a specific exception has been made. Strictly speaking visas are not required by law from UK nationals but are usually required in practice.

Foreigners may leave Spain when they wish from any recognised point of exit, with exceptions if criminal charges are pending, or if the Ministry of the Interior makes an order preventing departure on the grounds of national security, public order, public health, or the rights and liberties of Spaniards.

Deportation orders may be made for:

- being in Spain illegally (eg by failing to obtain or renew a residence permit);
- working without a work permit when one is required (Section 6.3), whether or not the foreigner has a residence permit;
- being implicated in activities which are contrary to public order or security (internal or external), or in activities which are contrary to Spanish interests or which might adversely affect Spain's relations with other countries;
- being convicted (not necessarily in Spain) of a crime which in Spain carries a penalty of imprisonment for more than one year;
- being guilty of delay or covering up or seriously misdeclaring personal circumstances to the Ministry of the Interior; and
- lacking lawful means of support or engaging in unlawful occupations.

A deportation order remains in effect for three years.

## 4.6 Driving licences and tourist plates

You may only drive on Spanish roads if you have a current valid driving licence *which you must carry with you when driving.* The driving licence must be shown to a police officer on request.

A British tourist may drive in Spain if he holds either a current international driving licence or a British driving lience with an official Spanish translation. An official translation can be obtained from the Spanish consulate in Britain or the British consulate in Madrid.

A resident of Spain, however, may only drive if he has a Spanish driving licence. There are different types of licence according to the type of vehicle to be driven. A 'B' licence covers domestic cars. A 'D' licence is needed to tow a trailer weighing in excess of 750 kg.

Holders of British driving licences can obtain the equivalent Spanish driving licence without sitting another driving test. The licence is usually obtained by using the services of a *gestor*. The first application must be accompanied with a photocopy of your passport and residence permit, current British licence and official translation, certificate of good conduct from the police, a certificate from the central registry in Madrid that no court proceedings are outstanding against you, a medical certificate from a doctor saying that you are a fit person to drive, and four photographs measuring 3.5 × 2.5cm which have your name, passport and residence permits on the back, and one of which is signed by the doctor.

The minimum age for driving is 18 years. A 'B' licence lasts for ten years between 18 and 45, for five years between 45 and 70, and for one year thereafter.

To renew a driving licence, you must produce a photocopy of your passport and residence permit, the previous Spanish licence, a medical certificate signed by a doctor, four photographs, one signed by the doctor, and a declaration that there have been no changes in your circumstances which affect your ability to drive.

The medical examination is carried out by a local doctor retained by the traffic authorities and takes only a few minutes. Disabled drivers can apply for a special licence to drive an adapted vehicle.

Traffic offences are usually dealt with by fixed penalties. These should either be paid or contested within ten days. There are discounts for prompt payment and surcharges for late payment.

Penalties are served on the address in your driving licence. If you have moved and not informed the authorities, the penalty is still regarded as having been properly served (and any surcharges correctly applied) even though you have not received details.

If you drive a UK registered car you must keep it legally roadworthy in the UK if your insurance in Spain is to remain valid. This includes display of a current UK road tax licence and current MOT certificates.

You can buy a car in Spain and register it with tourist plates, and obtain extensions to operate the car for up to five years. To do so you must bring into Spain 1 million pesetas a year in foreign exchange (or .5 million if retired), and you must not be engaged in any business. The extension of tourist plates is possible even if you later take out a *residencia*. The only identification needed is your passport. After five years you must pay the 33 per cent IVA to register the car on normal plates, or sell the car to another non-resident.

The RACE (*Real Automovil Club de España*) can provide specialist advice on this. There are some disadvantages. Like foreign registered plates, tourist plates must be sealed when you are absent from Spain for more than two months (though most owners ignore this law). To unseal the car you need to visit first the customs office, and then the *Guardia Civil*. Tourist plates have to be registered twice a year on 30 June and 31 December costing about 10,000 pesetas a year plus visits to *trafico*, which is the local car administration office run by the government. Tourist plates are unlikely to be as attractive as foreign plates for someone who spends less than six months a year in Spain.

## 4.7 Traffic laws

The police patrol cars are often called 'heavenly twins' as they hunt in pairs; one is usually a trained mechanic, the other a first aider, so they can be quite welcome. If an approaching car flashes you it is a warning that the 'heavenly twins' are around the corner.

Fines for speeding vary. For exceeding local speed limits, an excess of 10 per cent speed is fined 4000 pesetas, 20 per cent 8000 pesetas, and then by increasing amounts to a maximum of 29,000 pesetas if you are 60 per cent over the limit.

|  | Speed limit | |
|---|---|---|
|  | *kph* | *mph* |
| Motorways | 120 | 75 |
| Main roads, with hard shoulders on both sides | 100 | 62 |
| Others, in open country | 90 | 56 |
| Towns, villages | 60 | 37 |

The maximum speeds can be exceeded outside towns and villages by up to 20 kilometres per hour when overtaking, provided the other vehicle is travelling at below the maximum limit.

# Chapter 5

# Exchange Control Regulations in Spain

## 5.1 Exchange control

For most of the post-war period, Britain and Spain, like most European countries, protected their currencies by stringent exchange control regulations.

In Britain the main instrument was the Exchange Control Act 1947. This was suspended in 1979 and finally repealed in 1987. There is now no UK restriction on taking money out of the country to Spain. The dollar premium (effectively a currency tax of up to 30 per cent) has also been abolished.

In Spain complicated restrictions were introduced in 1938 and largely remain today, though modified. There is no problem for the Briton bringing sterling into Spain and converting it to pesetas, but there can be problems in converting it back to sterling.

Control exists by restricting what types of bank account you may hold. This is decided according to your residence. For this purpose, residence is not determined by whether you have a residence permit or are resident for the purposes of the property laws. It depends on where you have your home. If you have homes in Spain and Britain, it depends on where you spend more than six months. On first moving to Spain, you will be treated as a non-resident until you have lived there for at least 90 days.

Any bank will exchange banknotes or travellers' cheques into pesetas on the spot. Banks displaying the Eurocheque sign will advance pesetas to the cardholder to his authorised limit. Tourists therefore need have no bank account at all.

The exchange control authority in Spain is the *Dirección General de Transacciones Exteriores*, which is a department of the Ministry of Economy and Finance. However, some of the ministry's functions have been delegated to the Central Bank of Spain, which in turn delegates some of them to specific banks.

Any financial operation between a resident and non-resident (whether a company or a person) involves exchange control regulations. Breaking exchange control rules can result in severe penalties.

## 5.2 Bank accounts

A foreign resident will usually have a domestic peseta account (see Section 5.3) as his only current account in Spain. There are other accounts, however, which a foreigner in Spain may hold and these are summarised below:

- convertible peseta account
- non-resident foreign currency account
- internal peseta account.

### Convertible peseta account

This account may be credited with pesetas or foreign currency (which is immediately converted to pesetas). Convertible pesetas have either been authorised as such or have been transferred from another convertible peseta account. Convertible pesetas are used to buy Spanish property, investments and general supplies. They may be used to buy acceptable foreign currencies at the prevailing rate of exchange. Before 1 January 1981 there was a more complicated system of 'A' and 'B' accounts, which was much more restrictive.

### Non-resident foreign currency account

A non-resident may hold foreign currency in this account if the currency is recognised by the Bank of Spain. Payments into it may only be made by cheques or transfers from foreign banks, and not from foreign banknotes. Funds may be converted to other recognised currencies. Such funds are free of all Spanish exchange control regulations.

### Internal peseta account

This account cannot be used to hold, buy or sell foreign currency. It can be credited with receipts in internal pesetas of rent, dividends, interest and the proceeds of property sales, and with any amounts from other accounts held by non-residents. Payments out are limited to personal expenses of the account holder, to the purchase of property for his exclusive use, and to acquire shares in quoted Spanish companies.

Most Spanish current accounts attract a low rate of interest on credit balances.

## 5.3 Domestic peseta account

This account can be used without restriction to make payments in

Spain. However its convertibility for residents is limited. For 1989 the limits were:

- 350,000 pesetas per person per holiday outside Spain, without any limit on the number of trips;
- 300,000 pesetas per person per business trip, subject to an overall limit of 2.1 million pesetas;
- costs and expenses for medical treatment overseas without limit, and 100,000 pesetas per month per person for related personal expenses, subject to various rules;
- costs of education and related living expenses outside Spain without limit, and 'pocket money' of 25,000 pesetas a month, subject to various rules;
- subscriptions and similar payments to 25,000 pesetas a month;
- up to one-quarter of net earnings (subject to the employer's written confirmation); and
- maintenance payments to close relatives outside Spain to 50,000 pesetas a month.

## 5.4 Deposit and current accounts

The difference between deposit and current accounts is less marked in Spain than in Britain, as current accounts attract interest on credit balances, and the difference between types of account are governed more by exchange control regulations than interest rates.

Deposit accounts are usually used for small or short-term savings; larger amounts are kept in savings accounts which attract a higher rate of interest. The rate of interest is governed by the period for which the depositor contracts to leave the money. This must be six months, but is often for one or more years. In contrast, withdrawals may be made at any time from a deposit account, which, as a result, are often used like current accounts.

Interest on these accounts is credited twice a year.

## 5.5 Writing cheques

The laws regarding writing cheques were revised in 1986. Spanish law is now very similar to English law, but there are a few points which need to be remembered.

In Spain, as for much of the Continent, the roles of the decimal point and comma are reversed. Thus what we would write as 45,269.21 the Spaniards would write as 45.269,21.

When writing numbers, the 'and' goes in a different place. Thus 'two thousand, three hundred and forty-four' is written as 'two thousand, three hundred forty and four', *does mil trescientos cuarenta y cuatro*.

The date must be written entirely in words, not using a number for the day of the month. Thus 9 March is written *Nueve de Marzo*.

Cheques are valid for six months.

The payee instructions must be in the first line and read *páguese al portador por este cheque* or *páguese al* [name] *por este cheque* ('pay bearer by this cheque' or 'pay [name] by this cheque'). The words *por este cheque* are particularly important.

Cheques may be open or crossed, as in Britain. The words *y Cia* ('and company') may be written in the crossing to ensure that the sum is paid to the payee's account only.

## 5.6 Plastic money

Most credit and charge cards commonly used in the UK may also be used in Spain. The commonest is the Visa card which may be used anywhere which displays the Eurocheque card.

Cash can be drawn against credit cards up to the unused balance of the holder's personal limit.

## 5.7 Investment: introduction

The Spanish government generally encourages foreign investment in its industries, and has relaxed many restrictions in this area during recent years. However, there are some industries where foreign investment is restricted, namely defence, radio and television, gambling and air transport.

There are no particular incentives (or disincentives) for foreign companies. They are given an equal footing with Spanish companies.

Foreign investments can usually be freely repatriated, and dividends and other shares of profit may be remitted.

For direct investment in a company by external contribution (ie from a foreign source), approval from the Ministry of Economy and Finance is needed. If the investment exceeds 50 per cent of the company's equity, approval requires prior registration. No objection from the Ministry constitutes approval.

Otherwise prior authorisation is only required for public investors, and for private investors whose investment takes a form other than cash, eg contributing property or know-how.

For companies, an investment of 20 per cent or more is considered as the point at which the investor can influence a company's affairs.

There are no restrictions on investments in equity share portfolios and few on real estate.

## 5.8 Inward investment

Foreign investments may be made in one of four ways:

- foreign currency;
- equipment which has a foreign origin;
- technical assistance (such as foreign patents and manufacturing licences); or
- any other form which has been authorised by *Dirección General de Transacciones Exteriores*.

There are no special exchange rules for an investment which takes one of these forms:

- establishing a branch by non-resident persons or bodies;
- participating in a Spanish company;
- participating in a joint venture with a resident company or person;
- acquiring urban or country real estate;
- acquiring a portfolio of investments;
- loans of an investment nature which exceed five years; or
- other types of approved investment.

## 5.9 Registration of investment

All foreign investment must be notified to the Ministry of Economy and Finance and be evidenced by a public document. The stockbroker or *notario* is obliged to report such investments to the Foreign Investment Registry. Banks are obliged to report all foreign investments and movements of foreign capital to the Bank of Spain.

There are no restrictions on a company with foreign participation or a Spanish branch of a non-resident company borrowing from local sources.

Foreign loans up to 750 million pesetas by Spanish-resident individuals or bodies do not require authorisation with the Bank of Spain. Such a loan must last for at least one year. The residence requirement of this concession prevents it from being used by a Spanish-resident branch seeking a loan from its non-resident parent company.

Any increase in capital, or other change in the foreign investment, of a company with foreign participation must be for a specific investment project. Details of that project must be submitted to the *Dirección General de Transacciones Exteriores*.

Any type of foreign loan not included in the above requires the approval of the Bank of Spain. A company breaches Spanish exchange control law if it records such a loan to or from a non-resident before the approval is obtained.

Investments which take the form of technical assistance (including know-how, patents or management services) require the prior approval of the Ministry of Industry and Energy. The contracts themselves must be registered with the Ministry of Industry and Energy, and the related payments must be registered with the Ministry of Economy and Finance. In practice this last permission is usually obtained through banks authorised by the Bank of Spain.

## 5.10 Repatriation of funds

Capital and accrued profits can usually be repatriated with little difficulty provided:

the necessary tax clearance has been obtained; and
the original investment was properly registered (Section 5.9).

Routine payments which represent a fair proportion of the company's head office expenses may be remitted with authorisation. The capital and interest on foreign loans may be remitted overseas provided the necessary requirements for registration have been met.

The same restrictions apply to making distributions (such as dividends) to non-residents and repatriating the proceeds of a sale of an asset.

Every January each Spanish-resident branch of a non-resident company must file a declaration known as the *Cuenta de Enlace*, which details as at the previous 31 December:

- the capital and reserves;

- profit or loss for the year and the previous year;
- the balance owed to head office; and
- management charges and other contributions made to head office.

*Chapter 6*
# Working in Spain

## 6.1 Introduction

Even if your intention in moving to Spain is to relax, you may soon find that the life of sunbathing and tennis playing is not fully satisfying, and you either want to do some work or run your own business.

There is no restriction on either, but for employment you need a work permit. The rules apply equally whether working for a British or Spanish employer.

## 6.2 Self-employment

If you work on a self-employed basis you supposedly do not need a work permit under EC rules. Despite these rules a special residence and work permit are needed in Spain as Spanish rules have yet to comply with those of the EC.

You are required to join the Spanish social security service (see Chapter 7); obtain a trade licence known as the *licencia fiscal* and register for income tax and IVA.

If you wish to practise your profession, you will usually have to become a member of the appropriate professional college. A British qualification will usually give some exemptions, but a written examination will usually still be required.

You must be careful that your self-employment does not come to be regarded as employment, as could happen if you repeatedly work for the same person.

## 6.3 Work permits

All foreigners, including other EC nationals, need work permits, though this will change by 1992.

The first prerequisite to getting a work permit is to have a residence permit. You can apply for a work permit and residence permit at the same time, when you will be given just one document for both functions.

There are two types of work permit: a restricted permit and the normal work permit. A restricted permit lasts for only six months and cannot be renewed, but is available immediately. The normal work permit can take up to a year to process.

To obtain a normal work permit you need to produce:

- your passport;
- certificate of registration with the British consulate;
- a medical certificate;
- an entry visa (not required if your stay is for less than 90 days);
- seven small photographs *which must be in colour*; and
- two copies of your work contract.

It may also be necessary to obtain from the Spanish Ministry of Labour a certificate stating that there is no Spanish national available to do the job.

A work permit for an EC national lasts for five years; for others it lasts for one year and is renewed annually thereafter.

To renew a work permit you must produce:

- the previous permit and two photocopies;
- the residence permit and a photocopy (except if the residence permit is part of the work permit);
- another seven small photographs;
- the work contract with two photocopies;
- your last tax declaration with two photocopies;
- a certificate of good conduct from the local police, and two photocopies; and
- social security forms C1 and C2, with two photocopies of each.

Either in obtaining or renewing a work permit it may be necessary to use the services of a *gestor*.

These rules regarding work permits will be abolished in the 1990s under the Treaty of Rome.


## 6.4 Running a business

To run a business, other than as self-employment, you must get a licence, *licencia de apertura*, from the town hall. The licence is similar to the UK planning permission but is wider in scope.

The licence will only be granted if the authorities are satisfied that the premises are suitable for the proposed business, comply with planning permission and are safe and hygienic. Licences may be issued subject to conditions.

Other factors to be considered are:

- incorporation (see Section 6.5);
- special rules for business premises (see Section 6.6);
- employment laws (see Section 6.7).

It will usually be necessary to employ a Spanish lawyer to deal with these matters.

## 6.5 Incorporation

As in the UK, it is possible to be a sole trader, *empresa individual*, with no further formalities.

Those who wish to assume a corporate identity have a similar range of choices in Spain, namely:

- a partnership: *sociedad colectiva;*
- a joint venture with a Spanish company: *associación de empresas en participación;*
- a private limited company: *sociedad de reponsabilidad limitada,* usually abbreviated to SL;
- a public limited company: *sociedad anonima,* usually abbreviated to SA.

In a partnership, the partners all assume full personal liability for the partnership's debts. It is possible to form a limited partnership, *sociedad comanditaria,* in which non-participating partners may limit their liability (as in a UK limited partnership).

A private limited company must not have more than 50 shareholders or more than 50 million pesetas in issued share capital.

A public limited company must have at least three shareholders. All the share capital must be issued, and at least 25 per cent of its registered share capital must be paid up. The company may issue bearer shares or have registered shareholders. The requirement that half must be held by Spanish nationals was abolished in the 1970s. The directors need not be Spanish or even be resident in Spain.

## 6.6 Business premises

Business premises are governed by the Law of Industrial Leases (for an existing business which you are taking over) or the Law of Urban Leases (for a new business).

The main difference is that there is no statutory security of tenure under the Law of Industrial Leases; renewal is a matter of negotiation between the landlord and the tenant. The landlord is not obliged to renew at all. The problem can be mitigated by an appropriate contract with the landlord when the agreement is first made.

For a new business, the Law of Urban Leases gives the tenant security of tenure provided he has paid the rent and kept to the terms of the lease. The landlord may increase the rent only by the amount stated in the state-issued bulletin *Boletín Oficial*.

The Law of Urban Leases allows the tenant to sell his business. The tenant must notify the landlord of the proposed assignment and the sum asked for the assignment. The landlord may then exercise what is known as the 'right of redemption' and pay the same to the tenant to recover the premises regardless of why he wants it back. If he does not exercise the right, he must agree to the assignment and is entitled to a percentage of the amount paid for the assignment. If the business has been established since 1942, the percentage is 10 per cent; before 1942 it can be as high as 30 per cent. The percentage applies only to the premises element, not the sum paid for fixtures, fittings, stock and goodwill.

## 6.7 Employment laws

Spain's employment laws are very generous to the employee compared with those of the UK.

The standard working week is 40 hours. However, it is becoming common now to replace the traditional siesta with a shorter lunch break.

Of Spain's 13 million workers, less than 2 million belong to trade unions. Agreements with unions are legally binding as the minimum working conditions.

Wage levels have been lower than the UK, but are fast catching up.

The employer does not have to provide any pension scheme, but has to pay high rates of social insurance (Section 7.4).

Overtime may only be worked for up to 80 hours a year. Extra social insurance is payable for overtime.

All employees are entitled to 30 working days' paid holiday. Remember also that Spain has 15 national public holidays and usually one local public holiday. There are generous provisions for maternity and even paternity leave.

Employees are entitled to double salary for June and December. This presents no problem if you have agreed an annual salary, but if you have agreed a monthly salary, remember that there are 14 'months' in a Spanish employment year.

There are strict laws for dismissal and redundancy, breach of which attracts an 'indemnity' of up to 42 months' pay.

There is no compulsory retirement age in Spain, and dismissal for old age is only fair if you can demonstrate that the employee's age restricts his ability to do the job.

## 6.8 Branch offices

A branch, *sucursal*, of a foreign company must be registered with the Spanish Mercantile Office befeore it opens. Registration is conditional upon a successful application to the Director General of Foreign Transactions.

The application must provide full details of the parent company and details of its proposed business activities in Spain. A deed of constitution must be prepared. If this is approved, it is then registered and a capital contribution of foreign currency is paid.

Such a branch may then trade with few restrictions, including obtaining credit facilities and buying properties. It may buy shares in companies quoted on the Spanish Stock Exchange, but cannot otherwise buy shares in a Spanish company.

## 6.9 Accounting requirements

Every company must keep these records:

- journal, *diario*;
- balance sheet, profit and loss account, and detailed schedules, *inventarios y balances*; and
- minutes of directors' and shareholders' meetings, *actas*.

These must be kept in bound volumes, with limited exceptions for looseleaf books. Each page must be pre-stamped by the municipal authorities. Entries must be made in chronological order, be in Spanish and show amounts in pesetas. Only records which comply will be accepted by the authorities.

Spanish company law allows shareholders to inspect the accounting records with help if necessary.

Quoted companies must be audited by independent auditors. Private companies must appoint two auditors from their shareholders. The members need not be accountants.

The main accountancy body is the *Instituto de Censores Jurados de Cuentas*. Accounting and auditing standards for Spain in line with EC regulations are being drafted by the *Instituto*.

*Chapter 7*
# Social Security and National Insurance

### 7.1 Social security: introduction

Spain has a social security system supported by compulsory payments, similar to the UK system.

Generally, you will be paying either Spanish national insurance or UK national insurance, not *both*. Both countries offer a similar range of benefits, though not always of similar amounts.

Sometimes one country will pay benefit in the other. Under other circumstances one country will regard payments made under the other's system as counting towards the eligibility requirements of its own system.

Further details of the joint scheme are given in leaflets SA29 *Your Social Security, Health Care and Pension Rights in the European Community*. This covers all the EC countries.

Enquiries about the UK scheme may be made to:

Department of Social Security
Overseas Branch
Newcastle upon Tyne
NE98 1YX

When you write you should state:

- your full name;
- your date of birth;
- your national insurance number;
- your pension number if relevant.

Enquiries about the Spanish scheme can be made to:

Instituto Nacional de la Seguridad Social
Subdireccion General de Relaciones Internacionales
Padre Damian 4
Madrid 16
Spain

## 7.2 Liability for UK contributions: employees

Unless you are Spanish-resident, you remain liable to pay UK national insurance for at least the first 12 months of your stay in Spain.

An employee continues paying class 1 national insurance at the same rate and under exactly the same rules as a UK-based worker if:

- he is already paying national insurance in the UK;
- he is working temporarily in Spain;
- the employment in Spain is not expected to exceed 12 months; and
- he is not going to Spain to replace another employee who has completed his tour of duty there.

Under these conditions, the employer obtains from the Overseas Branch of the DSS (address above) a certificate of the employee's continuing liability to pay UK national insurance. To obtain the certificate, the employer must tell the DSS:

- the employee's name (including any maiden name);
- the employee's UK national insurance number;
- the employee's date of birth;
- the employee's address in Spain;
- details of any members of the employee's family who will be travelling with him to Spain;
- the employer's name and address;
- the name and address of the employer's Spanish representative;
- whether the employee is replacing another employee;
- the date on which the employee starts work in Spain; and
- the date on which the employee expects to stop working in Spain.

The certificate is sent to the employer who should give it to the employee to keep.

If the employment, though expected to last no more than 12 months, actually exceeds 12 months, the period of paying UK contributions may be extended by up to another 12 months. To do this the Spanish authorities must agree on application by the employer before the first 12-month period has finished. Application is made by completing form UK/E2 (available from DSS Overseas Department) and sending it to:

Dirección General de Seguridad Social Ministerio de Trabajo

Nuevos Ministerios
Madrid

There are special schemes for government employees and the crews of ships and aircraft.

Unless the conditions above are met, the employee will be liable to pay Spanish national insurance and be unable to continue UK national insurance.

## 7.3 Liability for UK national insurance: non-employees

If you are self-employed, you can elect whether to continue paying class 2 contributions voluntarily while in Spain. Such an election is advisable if your work in Spain is for short periods.

If you decide to stop paying class 2 contributions, you advise the local DSS office, and write to the DSS Overseas Branch advising them of your date of departure. If you have a national insurance card, it should be returned. Remember to cancel any direct debit to pay the contributions.

If you elect to continue paying contributions voluntarily, you can choose between paying class 2 and class 3 (voluntary) contributions. You can only continue paying class 2 contributions voluntarily if you will be gainfully employed overseas. Non-employees other than self-employed (such as the unemployed) may only be able to elect to pay class 3 contributions (see below).

If you do have a choice between the classes, you need to consider what entitlements to social security benefits you wish to keep. The position is summarised below:

| Entitled to | Class 2 | Class 3 |
|---|---|---|
| Sickness and invalidity benefits | yes | no |
| Maternity benefit | yes | no |
| Basic retirement pension | yes | yes |
| Widow's benefits | yes | yes |
| Child's special allowance | yes | yes |
| Unemployment benefit | no | no |

Death grant was abolished from April 1988.

UK social security benefit is only payable on your return to the UK.

If you have recently been an employee, you may still meet the elegibility requirements for UK social security benefits on your past record of class 1 contributions.

Class 2 or 3 contributions may only be paid:

if you have lived in the UK continuously for three years at any time;
if you have paid UK national insurance for at least three years (not necessarily continuously).

Application to pay class 2 or 3 contributions while overseas is made by completing form CF83 found at the back of leaflet NI38 available from any DSS office.

You may find that you are ineligible to pay any UK national insurance while in Spain.

Class 4 national insurance is effectively a second income tax paid by the self-employed. It does not count towards any social security eligibility. Class 4 liability ceases when you stop working in the UK.

## 7.4 Spanish social security contributions

If you are below pensionable age (65 for a man, 60 for a woman) you have to pay a monthly contribution of Spanish national insurance. The amount depends on whether you are married and whether you are working. When you reach pensionable age, you do not have to make monthly contributions. The rate comprises a general rate of 4.8 per cent plus any relevant additional compulsory charge thus:

| | | |
|---|---|---|
| unemployment insurance | 1.1 | per cent |
| professional education | 0.1 | per cent |
| employment solidarity fund | 0.28 | per cent |

If you work overtime, there is a further surcharge of 2 per cent for essential work and 4.8 per cent for non-essential work.

The employer pays 24 per cent of the salary to a high limit, and 6.7 per cent thereafter.

The documentation to arrange this is dealt with by the local branch of the Spanish Social Security, *Instituto Nacional de Previsión*. You should take your passport with you.

Spain provides social security (known there as the social insurance scheme) for unemployment, sickness, invalidity, maternity, industrial injury, retirement, widowhood, guardianship, parenthood and on death. UK contributions will generally count towards your entitlement in Spain.

## 7.5 Health care in Spain

As in the UK, health care in Spain is a mixture of state provision and private arrangement.

The genuine tourist will probably have medical insurance included as part of the holiday package. However, the non-resident still with tourist status should check his position more carefully. Hospital accommodation fees are generally lower than in Britain, but medical fees and medicines (largely imported) are more expensive.

Since Spain joined the EC, UK residents have been entitled to join the Spanish National Health Service and receive the same benefits as a Spanish national. For pensioners this can be arranged by the Overseas Department of the UK DSS who will send you a form UK/E17. This form can then be handed to the Spanish authorities for free membership of the Spanish Health Service.

If you are working and not yet of pensionable age, you must join the Spanish Health Service. Otherwise you have a choice. If you elect not to join, you must arrange adequate private health insurance. In practice many people belong to both the state and a private scheme.

Insurance can be arranged in the UK or Spain. In the UK insurance is offered by three companies: BUPA, PPP and Exeter Hospital Aid Society. Each offers a range of schemes depending on what level of cover you want.

In Spain there are over 300 companies that offer health insurance. Most are reputable but some are not, so it is advisable to have a policy checked by an independent insurance broker before signing. Many Spanish policies are limited to a specific hospital or area, or even specific doctors. This in itself is no particular disadvantage, though obviously it is essential to go to the hospital or area as stated on the policy.

Most Spanish policies now do not require you to pay the bill and make a claim. Often vouchers are provided with the policy which allow you to 'pay' the bill immediately. The policies usually cover the full cost of treatment, but this should be checked.

There are also variations between policies on whether there is cover for dental treatment, injuries sustained by accident, illness treated other than by surgery, extra beds for members of the family (eg parents of young children), consultation, X-rays and private rooms.

If going to Spain for more than three months for any reason, you must return your medical card to the Family Practitioner

Committee (Area Health Board in Scotland).

There are no circumstances under which the UK National Health Service will pay for treatment overseas.

## 7.6 Medical treatment in Spain

Generally the quality of medical treatment in Spain in both the private and public sectors is highly regarded. They are not without their problems, however. In March 1987 doctors in the state sector started a series of strikes for better pay and changes in the health system.

The state scheme guarantees free hospital accommodation and treatment therein. Medical treatment will only be provided under the EC Regulations by doctors practising under the National Social Security Institute (Instituto Nacional de la Seguriad Social, known as INSS).

There are detailed procedures to be followed and further information can be obtained from a Provincial Office (*Direction Provincial*) or local office (*Agencies*) of the INSS. Unless you follow these procedures you will be charged as a private patient.

Pensioners from the UK should obtain a *carnet de pensionista* issued by the INSS to obtain free medical care.

The state scheme covers treatment for medical conditions which existed before you moved to Spain. Medicines prescribed by the INSS doctor can be obtained from any chemist (*farmacia*). Unless you are a UK (or other EC) pensioner (in which case the medicines will be provided free), you will have to pay up to 40 per cent of the cost.

The main reason for maintaining private health insurance is for the 'five star' luxury of certain private hospitals, and to be treated in a hospital where English is spoken. St Bernard's Hospital in Gibraltar is an excellent hospital where English is the spoken language and is now freely available to Spanish residents. You should, however, check your policy to see that you are insured or be willing to pay the bill yourself.

You will probably have to pay for dental treatment, which is rarely available under the INSS scheme. These charges will *not* be refunded.

The pleasant climate and slower pace of life in Spain will also help to keep you in good health.

Having either established Spanish residence or a liability to pay under the Spanish social insurance scheme, your position on any return visit to the UK is the same as if you were a Spanish national visiting this country. You will be entitled to full treatment under the National Health Service during any visit to the UK. If your treatment is not an emergency measure, you will have to pay for it. Some Spanish health insurance policies cover treatment in the UK (and other countries).

## 7.7 Pensions

Having established an entitlement to either a UK or a Spanish old age pension, you can draw that pension in the other country. Unlike other social security payments it will be paid at the rate determined by the country in which you established your entitlement.

So if you are entitled to an old age pension in the UK, and then settle in Spain, you will receive a pension from the Spanish authorities but at a rate fixed by the UK authorities. This provision applies not only to the basic pension but also to increments based on the postponement of your retirement.

If you have paid contributions in both countries, you will receive a pension from both countries. Each country recalculates the contributions made in the other country to what they would have been had you not been resident there. The resulting pension is then reduced on a pro rata basis according to the actual value of contributions made in each country. The two pensions together may not exceed the higher of what each country would have paid had all your contributions been with that country.

Payments under the Spanish scheme do not count towards any pensions other than the basic NI retirement pension.

## 7.8 Unemployment benefit

Neither country pays unemployment benefit in the other, but each country recognises contributions made under the scheme run by the other for benefits.

In the UK, the benefit only arises from class 1 contributions paid by employees (and their employers). To claim in the UK it is necessary for you to have paid at least one class 1 contribution since your return to be eligible for unemployment benefit.

UK unemployment benefit cannot be paid for any period while you are in Spain unless you can demonstrate that you were in Spain seeking employment.

In Spain, UK class 1 contributions made in the 12 months prior to your arrival are taken into account for their scheme.

If you intend to work in Spain, you must obtain employment and a work permit to cover it *before* you go. (You may wish to seek advice about this from the embassy.) This means that unless you are a Spanish national and are returning to that country, you will not be able to look for work and get unemployment benefit while you are doing so. This provision applies to Spain until 1 January 1993.

There are special provisions which apply to members of your family and for full details you should write to the DSS Overseas Branch.

## 7.9  Sickness and invalidity benefit

UK invalidity benefit may be paid in Spain provided the usual UK conditions are met.

UK sickness benefit can be paid in Spain provided you meet the usual UK conditions, and also meet one of these conditions:

- you remain compulsorily insured under the UK scheme;
- your condition necessitates immediate treatment while staying in Spain, and within three days of the beginning of your incapacity you submit a certificate issued by a doctor to the Overseas Department of the DSS;
- you are authorised to return to a Spanish residence by the DSS having met the conditions for UK sickness benefit; or
- you are authorised by the DSS to go to Spain for medical treatment.

If you do not meet the conditions for UK sickness or invalidity benefit, your contributions will count towards the Spanish sickness or invalidity benefit.

If you qualify for both UK and Spanish sickness benefit, you will receive the benefit from the last country to which you made contributions.

If you are covered under the Spanish scheme while working in the UK, the Spanish scheme will pay benefit to you. If, however, you have paid at least one class 1 or class 2 contribution to the UK scheme while in the UK, you will receive UK benefit for which your Spanish contributions will count.

## 7.10  Maternity benefit

Since 20 June 1987, an employee who gives birth has been entitled (subject to some exceptions) to receive statutory maternity pay. The mother's entitlement depends on her being resident within the EC, and therefore includes Spanish-resident mothers. Statutory maternity pay is paid by the employer who reclaims it from the DSS.

Women who do not qualify for statutory maternity pay (because they are not employed or because they do not meet the employment conditions) are entitled to maternity benefit which comprises a grant and an allowance. The eligibility requirements can be satisfied by contributions from either the mother or her husband. As long as at least one of them continues making UK contributions, the benefit will be paid for any confinement in Spain.

A woman not liable to pay UK national insurance, but who has worked and paid contributions in the UK and who would have been entitled to benefit if she were in the UK, may still claim UK benefit provided that the other conditions of maternity benefit are met, and at least one of these conditions is satisfied:

- the woman's condition necessitates immediate treatment during a stay in Spain and within three days of the confinement she submits to the UK authorities a certificate of incapacity for work issued by the doctor who is treating her;
- the DSS has authorised the woman to go to a Spanish residence;
- for any reason, the woman is authorised to go to Spain to have the baby.

If a woman cannot claim under the UK system at all, she may claim under the Spanish scheme which will count any contributions made by the woman or her husband towards eligibility, provided that the mother or her husband has become subject to Spanish law since arrival.

A woman insured under the Spanish scheme will receive Spanish benefit in the UK under conditions which exactly mirror those for UK benefit. If the woman has paid at least one class 1 or class 2 contribution she becomes entitled to UK benefit for which her or her husband's Spanish contributions count towards eligibility.

If a woman is entitled to both Spanish and UK maternity benefit, she will receive the benefit from the country in which she gives birth. If she gives birth in neither country, she will receive benefit from the country to which she or her husband last made a contribution.

Other forms of maternity pay and all forms of paternity pay made by employers are contractual arrangements and are not affected by any of these provisions.

Section 1.14 gives advice on legal matters connected with births in Spain.

## 7.11 Industrial disablement benefit

Industrial disablement benefit is paid by both countries, each of which can pay it in the other country.

You are regarded as having had the accident in the country under whose scheme you are covered. So if you pay UK national insurance and have an accident while working in Spain, you will receive UK benefit.

The eligibility for benefit will be decided by the law of the country which governs the contract of employment, subject to two exceptions relating to industrial diseases. If you contract an industrial disease from work in one country only, your claim will be decided by the law of that country. If you contract an industrial disease from work in both countries, the entitlement will be determined by the country to which you last made a payment.

Industrial death benefit is paid to a widow whether she is in Spain or the UK. Similarly the child's allowance which attaches to this benefit remains payable even when the child is in Spain.

Spanish industrial death benefit also has an increase for children, and that increase is paid whether the children are in Spain or the UK.

## 7.12 Widow's benefit

A widow is entitled to receive widow's benefits in accordance with the same rules as for old age pensions (Section 7.7).

Where the widow is entitled to an addition for a child, that addition remains payable if the child is in Spain.

## 7.13 Orphan's benefit (UK guardian's allowance)

An insured person, or a child, who is ordinarily resident in either the UK or Spain can be treated as ordinarily resident in the other country as regards receiving UK guardian's allowance or Spain's orphan's benefit.

## 7.14 Child benefit

UK child benefit remains payable for the first six months of any temporary absence from the UK by the parent or child.

If the parents are working in Spain, child benefit remains payable while the parents are still insured under the UK scheme and the children are resident either in Spain or the UK (or another permitted country). If covered by the Spanish scheme, Spanish family allowances remain payable to families resident in either country.

If you are employed and entitled to another social security benefit from one country, you are entitled to child benefit/family allowance from the country paying you benefit. This means that you can receive benefits from both countries. This provision is unaffected by the residence of the family.

In other circumstances you will receive benefit only from the country under whose scheme you are insured, regardless of your family's actual residence. If one parent is working in the UK and is entitled to UK child benefit, Spanish law prevents the other parent claiming Spanish family allowance.

In any other circumstances where benefit could arise in both countries, benefit will be paid only by the country where the children are ordinarily resident.

Contributions under the Spanish scheme count towards entitlement to UK child benefit. Spanish family allowance is not contribution-based.


## 7.15  Death grant

A death grant is only paid by one country. The UK death grant has been abolished in respect of any death occurring after 5 April 1988. The flat-rate contributory grant was originally intended to pay towards the cost of funeral arrangements. However, the rate of the lump sum grant (a maximum of £30 for a person aged 18 or over) was universally acknowledged to be inadequate to cover the cost of even a very basic funeral (now estimated to be over £500). It appears that the new regulations will not allow the social fund funeral payment to be payable to anyone except a narrow band of claimants including those on supplementary benefit.

# Chapter 8

# Shedding UK Residence

## 8.1 UK residence

The emigrant and expatriate are usually hoping to cease to be both 'resident' and 'ordinarily resident' in the UK, to avoid UK income tax and capital gains tax on their worldwide income and capital gains. To succeed, one has to understand the meaning of the terms 'resident' and 'ordinarily resident'. Ordinary residence is explained in Section 8.7, and residence is explained below.

'Resident' in the UK has a very wide meaning. A tax year starts on 6 April and ends on the following 5 April. As a general rule, an individual will be resident in the UK in a particular tax year if:

1  he lives in the UK for more than six months in that year; or
2  he lives in the UK for more than three months on average over four consecutive tax years; or
3  he visits the UK even for just a few minutes, and has accommodation in the UK 'available' for his use.

The word 'available' does not mean that the individual owns residential accommodation, nor does it imply a legal right of occupation. Merely having a place set aside for his use (eg, a bedroom in someone's home) could be sufficient. A house which you own, but which is let commercially, is not 'available' accommodation. Not using available accommodation on a particular visit is irrelevant. Simply setting foot in the UK can trigger residence for tax purposes.

The above rules may be overridden by double taxation agreements where the individual is resident both in the UK and in another country. The way the UK/Spain double tax treaty works is discussed in Section 8.4.

There is an exception where an individual is engaged overseas full time in a trade, profession, vocation, office or employment, provided that no part of his duties are carried out in the UK (with minor exceptions in the case of company employees). Such an individual will be non-resident, even though he has a property available to him in the UK. This exception covers a person working in a self-employed capacity so long as the activities are genuinely full time, ie the number of hours worked are similar to those of a national of the country of residence with a full-time business or employment.

It is important to note that such an individual must either:

1 be working full time in a trade, profession or vocation and *no part* of the trade must be carried on in the UK; or
2 be working full time in employment overseas and any duties performed in the UK are *merely incidental* to the overseas duties.

In either case, having available accommodation will *not* be a factor in determining resident status.

However, the Inland Revenue take a harsh line on the definition of 'merely incidental duties' and the more senior the employee, the harder it is to establish that UK duties are 'merely incidental'. Visiting the UK to report to your boss is usually regarded as incidental. Attending a board meeting, however, is not regarded as incidental by the Inland Revenue. The Revenue will look at the quality of the duties undertaken in the UK rather than the time spent on them to determine whether or not they are merely incidental.

A husband and wife are looked at separately. Thus it is possible for the husband to be non-resident while his wife is a UK resident. For example, if the husband is in genuine full-time employment overseas he will be regarded as non-resident. On the other hand, his wife, if she is not employed overseas, will be a UK resident and therefore liable to tax on her income worldwide (even though she is living with him), if the couple have the use of the family property in the UK and she spends a few minutes in the UK.

Figure 1 on page 114 will help you through the maze of rules on residence. However, it must be stressed that the residence rules are not precisely defined and your individual circumstances always need to be considered. In particular, if you plan your life so as to keep marginally within 1 and 2 above, or so as to remain outside the UK for a single tax year and a day or two on either side, there is a significant risk that the Revenue could successfully challenge your anticipated non-resident status.

It is important to keep a detailed record of all your time spent in each country, showing dates of arrival and departure, and places stayed at. This could be vital evidence in the event of a dispute, but also read Section 8.9.

## 8.2  UK residence maze

To help you work out whether or not you are likely to be a resident in the UK in a tax year, follow the maze below:

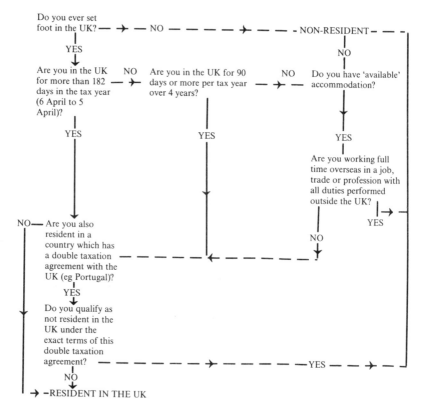

**Figure 1**   UK residence maze

## 8.3  The tax maze

Even if you are 'resident' in the UK, your employment earnings may still be free of tax. Follow the maze shown in Figure 2.

## 8.4  The UK/Spain double tax treaty

The UK/Spain double taxation agreement was signed on 21 October

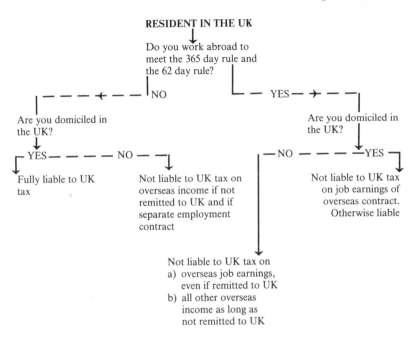

**RESIDENT IN THE UK**

Do you work abroad to meet the 365 day rule and the 62 day rule?

NO → Are you domiciled in the UK?

YES → Are you domiciled in the UK?

YES — Fully liable to UK tax

NO — Not liable to UK tax on overseas income if not remitted to UK and if separate employment contract

NO — Not liable to UK tax on a) overseas job earnings, even if remitted to UK b) all other overseas income as long as not remitted to UK

YES — Not liable to UK tax on job earnings of overseas contract. Otherwise liable

**Figure 2**  *The tax maze*

1975. A copy may be obtained from HM Stationery Office under reference SI 1976/1919. It has a 'tie breaker' clause that comes into operation if you are resident both in the UK under our rules and in Spain under theirs. The purpose is to determine in which country you will be regarded as resident for the purpose of taxes covered by the agreement – it *cannot* be both.

The agreement often works as follows:

- If you are resident in both countries according to each country's domestic rules, you are deemed to be resident in the country in which you have *a permanent home* available to you.
- If you have permanent homes available in both countries, you are deemed to be resident in the country that is your *centre of vital interests*, ie the country with which your personal and economic relations are the closest.
- If this test is indeterminate, you are deemed to be resident in the country in which you have an *habitual abode*, but if you have one in both countries, you are deemed to be resident in the country of which you are a *national*. UK nationals will at this point be regarded as UK residents.

## 8.5 Form P85

On leaving the UK, you should obtain a form P85, complete it and forward it to your tax office. If you cease to be resident in the UK during a tax year, you are still entitled to full personal allowances for the whole tax year and may therefore receive a tax refund. Be careful in completing this form; professional advice should be sought. The form includes such questions as:

1  What is the date you left, or intend to leave the UK?
2  What is your nationality?
3  If you are a British subject:
   – On what grounds do you claim this status?
   – Where were you born?
4  How long have you lived in the UK before your departure?
5  To what country are you going?
6  Do you intend to stay abroad permanently? Yes/No
   If 'No', will you be staying abroad for at least 12 months from 5 April following your departure?
7  If you are married, is your wife going too? Yes/No
   If 'Yes', please give the date or intended date of her departure.
8  Please list below the periods you and your wife (if you are married) expect to spend in the UK during the next three years.
9  Will either you or your wife (if you are married) have any accommodation in the UK while you are away? Yes/No
   If 'Yes', what is the type of accommodation and the address? Do you own the property? Yes/No
   If 'Yes':
   – Are there any loans or mortgages on the property? Yes/No
     If there are, give full details. Include account/roll numbers, names of lenders and amount outstanding for each loan.
   – Do you pay loan interest net after tax relief? Yes/No
   – Do you intend to return to the property as your sole or main residence within four years of the date of your departure? Yes/No
10  Will either you or your wife (if you are married) be receiving rents, premiums or other income from property in the UK? Yes/No
   If 'Yes', give the following details of each of the properties concerned:
   – The type of payments (rent, etc) and whether let furnished or unfurnished

- The approximate income each year (£)
- The address of the property
- Whether you (or your wife) will be receiving the income direct (in the UK or elsewhere); if so, give the name and address of the payer
- Whether you (or your wife) will be receiving the income through an agent who manages the property for you; if so, give the name and address of the agent (or payer if the agent lives outside the UK).

11 Will either you or your wife (if you are married) have any other source of income in the UK after you have left? Yes/No If 'Yes', please give details.
If you will not be working abroad you need not answer questions 12 to 18. Go straight to question 19.

12 If you are taking up employment abroad, give the name of your employer and his address. If you are employed by the UK government, give the name of the Department and the type of job.

13 How will you be paid for your work? For example, will you be paid abroad or in the UK, by credit to your account or otherwise?

14 If any part of your pay is to be paid through an office or agent in the UK, please give the full name and address of the payer.

15 Will your employment be full-time? Yes/No

16 Do you hold a separate contract for your employment overseas? Yes/No

17 What is the length of your contract?

18 What is, or will be, the type of employment abroad and will any duties be carried out in the UK (if so, give full details of these duties)?
If your overseas work is on a days on/days off rota, please give details and say where you expect to spend the days off.

19 If you are not going abroad to work, say why you are leaving the UK.

20 Life assurance
If you move abroad, your entitlement to pay premiums net of tax relief may be affected. Please give below full details of all the premiums you will continue to pay after leaving the UK on policies taken out before 14 March 1984.
Include your wife's premiums if she is also leaving the UK. Do not include premiums paid on your behalf by your wife if she is staying in the UK.
- Name of insurance company

- Policy number
- Premiums payable in year to 5 April 19 .... £ ......
21 Did you notify your insurance company of your date of departure from the UK? Yes/No

Completion of the Inland Revenue form P85 will enable the Inspector of Taxes to make a preliminary assessment of your likely residence status while you are overseas. However, it is usual Inland Revenue practice to regard you as *provisionally* not resident and not ordinarily resident from the date of departure. However, if you intend to make a large capital gain on leaving, read Section 9.5. If you are employed by a UK company, ask the company to obtain a 'Nil Tax' (NT) coding to be used against your salary while you are abroad.

During the first three years abroad, the Inland Revenue may write to you requesting confirmation of your intention to remain overseas, and great care should be taken in replying.

## 8.6 The date of non-residence

By concession, you are normally regarded as becoming non-resident the day after you leave the UK, even though this may be in the middle of a tax year. A tax year starts on 6 April and ends the following 5 April. This concession applies for both income tax and capital gains tax.

Technically, however, your UK residence extends for the *entire* tax year, ending 5 April after you leave the UK. The Inland Revenue can refuse to apply the concession if they consider that you have timed your departure, or entered into a transaction, specifically to avoid capital gains tax. It can therefore be dangerous, for example, to realise an enormous capital gain on shares or property or on a business soon after you leave the country. It is safer to sell your assets in the tax year *following* your departure from the UK.

## 8.7 Ordinary residence

The UK recognises two forms of residence: residence and ordinary residence. This is a distinction made by few other countries. Accordingly double taxation agreements (such as UK/Spain) do not cover the ordinary residence rules.

Ordinarily resident is not defined in the Taxes Act, but is generally understood to denote the status of someone who is usually resident as opposed to extraordinarily or casually resident for one tax year only.

You will normally be ordinarily resident in the UK if you spend more than three months in the UK on average over four tax years. This concept is very important for *capital gains tax* as you have to be *both* not resident and not ordinarily resident in the UK to be free from UK capital gains tax. You only have to be not resident to avoid UK income tax on income other than UK income.

Usually, the Inland Revenue accept that if you are not resident in the UK for three *complete* and *consecutive* tax years, you are not ordinarily resident from 6 April following your departure from the UK. By concession, they might regard the date of commencement of not ordinarily resident to be the date of departure.

You can obtain provisional clearance as being not ordinarily resident if you produce evidence to show that your departure from the UK will be for at least three years. (In other words, your intention to leave the UK permanently is important.) Such evidence would include the disposal of UK accommodation and the availability of a permanent home overseas. The provisional clearance will usually have effect from the day after you leave the UK. You can lose your provisional clearance if you return to the UK before three complete tax years have elapsed.

If you cannot provide such evidence, the Revenue will wait until after the three complete tax years have passed and then decide, based on what has happened. The clearance, if given, can be effective from the tax year after you left the UK.

The three-year period mentioned above is an arbitrary period deemed by the Inland Revenue to be sufficient to decide whether or not you have made a 'distinct break' from the UK.

Finally, remember that even if you obtain provisional tax clearance, if you return within the three-year period you will forfeit the exemption. It does not matter why you returned; returning because of the illness of a loved one will not be a reason for avoiding residence status. There is no compassionate exemption from tax.

## 8.8 Retaining a UK home

If you are trying to become both not resident and not ordinarily resident, keeping a UK home which is available for your use can be a major obstacle. You can take lots of steps to ensure you are protected from being a UK resident, even though you continue with your UK home. The most typical route for avoiding UK residence status is protection under the double tax treaty. Alternatively, you may be working full time in Spain, when your UK home does not affect UK residence status.

But the home is a major problem when it comes to UK ordinary residence. The UK/Spain double tax treaty says nothing about ordinary residence, and thus cannot offer protection. It can therefore be argued that an individual can be:

resident in the UK because of available accommodation
*but* not resident, as the UK/Spain double tax treaty overrides
*but* ordinarily resident in the UK because of available accommodation.

In such a case, the existence of available accommodation can lead to someone being classed as not resident but ordinarily resident in the UK, and hence liable to UK capital gains tax. So retaining a home could lead to a large tax liability.

If you have a full-time job overseas in Spain, the position is less clear, but it is often better not to have any accommodation available in the UK if there is a large UK capital gains tax liability at stake. Professional advice should be sought.

### 8.9 'How do they know where I am resident?'

We are often asked how the tax men of the world can find out whether or not you are resident in their country, and how they can then tax you. There are many points to be aware of.

In most countries it is your responsibility to make yourself known to the tax authorities if you are tax resident. If you are caught not declaring your tax residence, you can be fined, or even gaoled.

There is usually a huge amount of information which is automatically passed to your new country's tax authority. This might include yacht registration, becoming a company director, buying a property, receiving bank interest. Often you need a tax reference number just to open a bank account. Under a new agreement being supported by all members of the OECD each member state will *automatically* pass information to the other, and help collect the other country's tax debt. So if you move from the UK to Spain, for example, your UK tax inspector might in the future be required to send full details of your assets, tax history etc, to the Spanish tax man. Note that at the time of writing, this agreement has not yet been ratified or implemented. However, the UK/Spain double tax treaty enables information to be passed to the other country, but not on an automatic basis.

Many non-residents totally confuse tax residence with two other kinds of residence – immigration and exchange control. The definitions of tax residence, immigration residence and exchange control residence are normally completely different.

Being non-resident for exchange control or immigration purposes has nothing to do with your tax residence. Your tax residence is determined by completely different rules, and therefore you must make no assumptions, but take good professional advice in order to understand your position.

It is no good saying to the tax man in the UK that you are resident in Spain unless it is true. He will immediately ask for your tax identification number in Spain so that he can make contact to check out your story (and vice versa).

As you wonder how they can tell where you have been for the last 183 days (or whatever) as your passport is never stamped, think about the massive trail of paperwork which you leave behind you – telephone bills, electricity bills, bank statements, credit cards, parking fines, correspondence with professional advisers or files with doctors/dentists etc. All stand by to give evidence of your whereabouts on a daily basis. Airline manifests are not sacrosanct. In Spain some time ago American Express were forced to disclose to the tax authorities the names of all holders of their Gold Card. Most tax men have power to obtain this kind of information direct from third parties. Computers are phenomenal at storing and retrieving information easily.

Try firing your gardener, or divorcing your wife, upsetting a neighbour, or falling out with a business partner. These people are well known for shopping 'ghosts' (individuals who are tax resident in a country but never declare themselves). In many countries there is a system of 'denunciation' where individuals may be rewarded for passing on information to the tax or rating authorities.

Most reasonably sophisticated tax authorities have the right to interview you, and possibly your spouse. Quite often the onus of proof can be placed on the taxpayer, rather than the tax inspector.

Moreover, if they have not asked the right questions during your lifetime, your nearest and dearest may find that when your death certificate is filed an inspector of taxes becomes extremely interested in how you managed to die in his country when you do not have a tax file number! You, of course, are not too interested at this point. But your wife may find that your estate disappears into paying large back taxes, penalties and interest.

Finally, if you are caught, your assets can be frozen in your country, making you bankrupt and, under new OECD rules being introduced, your tax debts can be chased into other OECD countries.

Take good professional advice to avoid tax legally – there is no need to go the illegal route.

### 8.10 Tax planning points on UK residence

1 Avoiding UK residence can be easy. If you work full time in Spain, it is unlikely that you are resident in the UK.

2 Avoiding ordinary UK residence is more difficult but can be done by not having available accommodation or by working full time in Spain.

3 Remember, no protection from inheritance tax or wealth tax is given by the double tax treaty; other steps must be taken to avoid these taxes.

4 Completing the form P85 on leaving the UK needs care. Innocent looking questions can have a major influence on your tax position. Advice should be sought in completing this form.

5 Do not rely on Inland Revenue concessions on residence status. They will almost certainly be denied if you are trying to use them as protection against a tax bill.

6 Note that husband and wife's residence may be determined by reference to the residence status of either. If your wife is resident you may also be deemed resident even though you only visit the country in question occasionally.

7 There is often a period when an individual is a fiscal nomad: not being tax resident anywhere. This can be the position after leaving the UK, but before officially becoming resident in Spain. Advice should be sought as to how this can be used to advantage.

8 If you are self-employed (a sole trader or a partnership), there can be considerable tax savings in careful timing of the cessation of trading. Professional advice must be sought.

*Chapter 9*
# UK Capital Gains Tax

## 9.1 Introduction

UK capital gains tax used to be charged at a flat rate of 30 per cent on the gain made on the disposal of 'chargeable assets'.

From 6 April 1988, any capital gains made are added to your income and tax paid at the appropriate income tax rate (or rates) of 25 and/or 40 per cent. If the asset was purchased prior to 31 March 1982, the original cost of the asset is ignored and the market value at 31 March 1982 substituted. A chargeable asset includes all assets unless they are specifically exempt (and these exempt assets are listed in Section 9.3).

Any losses which arise on the disposal of an asset are offset against chargeable gains made in that same tax year. If the losses exceed the gains, the unrelieved loss may be carried forward indefinitely against any future capital gains. The unrelieved losses cannot be carried back, nor can they be offset against any income liable to tax – they can only be offset against capital gains.

A special allowance is given to adjust for inflation (called 'indexation allowance'). The first £5000 of the gains in a tax year is exempt, and the balance is liable to capital gains tax at your income tax rates.

## 9.2 How capital gains tax is calculated

### Example
As an example, John Smith purchased a property in July 1984 which he let to a tenant. The property cost him £65,00, plus legal costs of £1500. In July 1989 he sells the house for £132,000, and has to pay the estate agent £3000 plus VAT of 15 per cent (another £450) and legal fees of £2000 plus VAT of £300. His capital gains tax is calculated as:

| | | |
|---|---:|---:|
| Sale price July 1989 | | £132,000 |
| Less: estate agent | | (3,450) |
| legal costs | | (2,300) |
| | | £126,250 |
| Purchase price – July 1984 | £65,000 | |
| Legal fees | 1,500 | |
| Indexation allowance (estimated) | 15,835 | (82,335) |
| (see 9.6) | | |
| Chargeable gain | | 44,215 |
| Less: Exempt (see 9.4) | | (5,000) |
| Taxable gain | | 37,615 |
| Capital gains tax due – at say 40% | | £15,046 |

This example assumes John Smith is a resident in the UK. Had he spent money on improving the property, that also would have been deductible.

Had he owned the asset prior to 31 March 1982, the market value as of 31 March 1982 would have been substituted for the original cost figure.

### 9.3 Assets exempt from capital gains tax

The following assets are not liable to capital gains tax (CGT).

1 An individual's only or main private residence. There are special rules described more fully in Section 10.8.
2 One other residence occupied rent free and without other consideration by a dependent relative, where occupied prior to 5 April 1988.
3 Chattels which are wasting assets, unless used in a business. A wasting asset is one which has a predictable life of less than 50 years. Chattels are tangible movable property such as coins, furniture, works of art, fur coats, yachts, greyhounds etc. Currency is not exempt unless it is sterling or foreign currency for personal use while abroad.
4 Non-wasting and business chattels where disposal proceeds of an individual item do not exceed £3000. Items comprising a set or collection are treated as individual assets unless they are sold to the same or connected persons, in which case the sale is treated as one sale arising on the occasion of the last sale.

5  Gilt-edged securities, local authority bonds and qualifying corporate bonds. A qualifying corporate bond is a bond issued by a UK listed company (or one traded on the USM) denominated in sterling.

6  Save As You Earn contracts, savings certificates and premium bonds.

7  Prize and betting winnings.

8  Private motor cars including veteran and vintage cars.

9  Sterling currency and foreign currency for an individual's own spending and maintenance of assets abroad.

10  Decorations of valour if disposed of by the original holder or legatees but not by a purchaser.

11  Compensation or damages for personal or professional wrong or injury.

12  Life assurance policies but only in the name of the original owner or beneficiaries or a person who received the policy as a gift from such a person.

13  Gifts of assets that are considered by the Treasury to be of national, historic or scientific interest, but breach of any conditions imposed will nullify the CGT exemption.

14  Gifts to charities.

## 9.4  The annual exemption

For 1989/90, the annual exemption is £5000. A loss made in a tax year must be offset against gains of that same year, but losses brought forward need not be set against gains covered by the exemption. In the year of marriage, both husband and wife each have a £5000 exemption (total £10,000) and will each have a £5000 exemption after marriage under new rules being introduced in 1990. Where the husband dies, or there is a separation or divorce in the tax year, the usual rules apply to the date of death (or separation or divorce), but then the wife gets a full exemption for the rest of the year as if it were a separate tax year.

## 9.5  Husband and wife

Gains of a husband and a wife are calculated separately, but then totalled and charged on the husband, unless one of them applies for separate assessment (though this will never reduce the amount of tax payable). Either husband or wife can elect for his or her losses to be carried forward instead of being set against the other's gains. Disposals between husband and wife in a tax year when they are living together are not chargeable. The acquiring spouse is treated as having acquired the asset when the other spouse acquired it, at its original cost plus indexation allowance to the date of transfer.

A husband's and wife's residence status are determined independently, and they are taxed as single persons if one is resident in the UK and the other is not. If they are still living together (even though one may be resident in the UK, and the other not resident), transfers from one spouse to the other are free of capital gains tax. In a famous case (*Gubay* v *Kington*), the tax man tried to argue that the normal exemption on disposal of assets between spouses did not apply where one was not resident and the other resident. The House of Lords ruled against the Revenue. Thus it appears that if a husband transfers all his assets to his non-resident (and not ordinarily resident) wife, and she sells them free of capital gains tax, the tax can be avoided. Professional advice must be sought in this area.

However, under the *Furniss* v *Dawson* principles, this tax avoidance method would be in doubt. The *Furniss* v *Dawson* tax case was a major victory for the Inland Revenue, and probably their best – and certainly favourite – win this century. The case established a principle that 'artificial arrangements' entered into solely to avoid tax can be set aside in certain circumstances and the tax man can therefore tax the individual as if those 'arrangements' never took place. Beware!

## 9.6 Indexation allowance

This is a form of relief for inflation. It is usually based on the cost price, except that where the asset was purchased before 31 March 1982 and disposed of after 6 April 1985, the taxpayer can claim that the indexation relief should be based on the market value of the asset at 31 March 1982 (which is normally above cost). This only gives you a higher indexation allowance – you cannot use the value at 31 March 1982 as the original cost of the asset in calculating the capital gain. Any claim to use the 31 March 1982 figure for indexation must be made within two years from the end of the tax year in which the disposal was made.

If the indexation allowance creates a loss, it can be offset against other gains (or carried forward). This only applies to disposals after 31 March 1985.

## 9.7 Retirement relief

Up to £125,000 of capital gains can be free of all UK tax (or £250,000 for husband and wife) on 'retirement'. Fifty per cent of the gains between £125,000 and £500,000 can also be free of capital gains tax. There are many traps and conditions, and the details are spelled out in Appendix 2.

## 9.8 Roll-over relief: shares

Where a taxpayer exchanges his shares (or debentures) to another company in exchange for the *issue* of new shares or debentures in that other company, no capital gains tax is payable if:

- the new company will hold at least 25 per cent of the shares of the old company; or
- the new company issues the shares (or debentures) as a result of a general offer to the shareholders of the old company, and will have control of the old company.

and it can also be shown that the exchange was carried out for bona fide commercial reasons and does not form part of a scheme or arrangement one of the main purposes of which is the avoidance of capital gains tax.

The Inland Revenue will give advance clearance on any proposed share roll-over transactions.

Note that roll-over is available into debentures (ie loan stock) as well as into shares.

If the taxpayer subsequently sells the new shares (or the debentures are repaid for cash) while he is non-resident, and not ordinarily resident, no UK capital gains tax would be payable (see Section 9.10). If some cash were received, as well as shares, partial roll-over would be due.

If the debentures (loan stock) have conversion rights to shares, the tax would not be payable on conversion. Tax is only due when cash is received.

## 9.9 Roll-over relief: business assets

Usually on selling a business asset owned personally (eg a freehold interest), you will be liable to capital gains tax at 40 per cent of the gain. Any expenditure incurred in acquiring the asset may be deducted (including stamp duty, legal costs etc), and you will be eligible for indexation relief which is a kind of relief for inflation. The tax is payable on 1 December following the tax year in which the gain was made.

Any gain made by a limited company on selling trading assets is also liable to corporation tax. Any improvement costs can be deducted against the sale proceeds.

Roll-over relief can be used as a half-way house to avoid UK capital gains tax by 'rolling over' the gain into a new asset while still a UK resident. On later becoming a non-resident, the asset can then be sold tax free. This is so even though the original gain was rolled over in a tax year when the taxpayer was both resident and ordinarily resident in the UK. Roll-over relief is often poorly understood by professional advisers. Full details of the relief are set out in Appendix 3. Careful advice is needed.

## 9.10  Avoiding capital gains tax: the general rules of non-residence

This section (and Section 9.11) set out the UK capital gains tax position for someone going to live *anywhere* outside the UK. These rules are also relevant for someone going to live in Spain.

The definitions of 'resident' and 'ordinarily resident' are to be found in Chapter 8. For UK domiciled individuals liability is as follows:

| UK domiciled | Capital gains tax liability |
|---|---|
| Resident | UK capital gains tax due on *all* assets throughout the world |
| Non-resident and not ordinarily resident | *Not liable* even if the assets are located in the UK (unless assets used for a trade in the UK – see next section). |

By concession, an individual leaving the UK is treated as non-resident the day after he has left the UK. This concession can be refused if the Revenue think tax has been deliberately avoided. It is therefore safer to realise capital gains in the tax year *after* you have left the UK (ie the year starting 6 April after you have left).

Note that the effective date a capital gain is realised is on the making of a contract – which in some cases can even be before a formal unconditional exchange of contracts – not on completion. 'Arrangements' made to sell an asset while in the UK – even though they are not legally enforceable – have been held to have been the effective date of disposal. Remember also that the Inland Revenue have the right to see all correspondence, memos etc, leading up to a contract, and they *often* request such documents.

If you realise a capital gain in the tax year you leave the UK and before the date you leave, the gain is definitely liable to UK capital gains tax, subject to the annual exemptions and other exemptions mentioned above.

To avoid UK capital gains tax, you have to be not resident and not ordinarily resident. Returning within three tax years of leaving will normally forfeit the exemption from capital gains tax. You need to be non-resident for three complete tax years.

There is a possible exception; if you have a full-time job overseas, and you are absent for a complete tax year, the Revenue's normal practice is to treat you as both not resident and not ordinarily resident in that year. However, you must have a genuine job full time overseas, and this is a concession which can be withdrawn by the Inland Revenue if they believe it is applied mainly to save tax! Furthermore it was introduced for income tax purposes and you should be wary of relying on it if you intend to realise a large capital gain.

### 9.11 A trap: assets used in a trade

*If you own an asset used in a UK trade, and the asset is situated in the UK, then even if you become not resident and not ordinarily resident, you will remain liable for capital gains tax.*

### Example

Mr and Mrs Lowes owned a successful freehold nursing home, which they operated as a partnership. They left the UK in February 1989, leaving a manager in charge of the home. In May 1989, the manager agreed to buy the nursing home giving the Lowes a capital gain of £430,000. Unfortunately Mr and Mrs Lowes *remain liable* for UK capital gains tax, even though they are both not resident and not ordinarily resident.

The reason they are liable is that section 12 of the Capital Gains Tax Act 1979 continues to tax a gain made on:

- assets situated in the UK; and
- where those assets are used in a trade. This would include business premises, work-in-progress or goodwill; and
- where the trade is conducted through a branch or agency in the UK.

Thus a partner disposing of an interest in assets used in the UK partnership would remain liable to UK capital gains tax. Even then, you should note that the capital gains tax is only chargeable in respect of a *trade*, not a profession. Unfortunately, there is no definition of a profession. It appears that training and examinations are an important test, and some code of professional honour. The courts have suggested that a journalist, editor, auctioneer, barrister and actress all exercise a profession, but not an insurance broker or stockbroker. However, this is not clear.

It is also worth pointing out that letting a UK property, held as an investment, is *not* a trade, and therefore not liable to be taxed by this trap. Even disposal of short-term holiday lettings – regarded as a trade for some sections of the Taxes Act – is *not* caught by this section of the Capital Gains Tax Act.

If you can't avoid the tax based on any of the above points, there are some other tax planning hints set out below.

### Tax planning

Mr and Mrs Lowes could have avoided UK capital gains tax by one of two methods.

1  *Incorporation.* If the business had been incorporated, the property could have been transferred to the new company or left in their own names and let (at a market rent) to the company. In either case, the sale of the shares and/or the nursing home freehold would have been free of UK capital gains tax if sold in the tax year after leaving the UK, provided that the Lowes remain both not resident and not ordinarily resident.

2  *Renting the freehold.* An alternative way would have been for the Lowes to let the nursing home to the manager. He signs a lease, paying a market rent. Later, having left the UK, established non-residence and non-ordinary residence, they could have sold the rental property to him free of UK capital gains tax.

There is one word of caution about such tax planning. There have been several tax cases (and, in particular, *Furniss* v *Dawson*) which enable the Revenue to ignore a series of transactions which have no real commercial purpose, other than the avoidance of tax, and impose tax as if they have not occurred.

### 9.12  Avoiding both UK capital gains tax and Spanish tax

This chapter has explained the classic methods of avoiding UK capital gains tax, but clever avoidance of UK tax could end up becoming a case of 'out of the frying pan and into the fire'. You also have to avoid paying Spanish tax on your gain.

There are several ways of achieving this; for example, by being a fiscal nomad for a few months. Alternatively, you can make your capital gains disposal while in a period when you are living in Spain *but* resident neither in Spain nor in the UK. Professional advice should be sought to ensure that all taxes are properly avoided.

## 9.13 The special rules under the UK/Spain double tax treaty

The general rules outlined in Sections 9.10 and 9.11 can be overridden by Article 13 of the UK/Spain double tax treaty, dated 21 October 1975.

The double tax treaty provides considerable protection from UK capital gains tax if you are a resident of Spain in a tax year when the disposal is made. Remember that making 'arrangements' to sell an asset before leaving the UK can be held to be the effective date of sale, even though the contract was signed in a tax year when you are resident in Spain. If you are resident in a tax year both in Spain and in the UK, the tie breaker rules set out in Section 8.4 come into play to determine in which country – UK or Spain – you are to be a resident for tax purposes, as the Double tax treaty states you *cannot* possibly be resident of *both* countries.

Assuming, therefore, that you have not made any 'arrangements' to sell before you leave the UK, and that you sell in a UK tax year when you are truly a Spanish resident, the double tax treaty sets out the rules for taxing a capital gain. The double tax treaty rules can be used to *override* the rules set out in Sections 9.10 awnd 9.11 above. However, the protection is in fact a very limited one since in most cases you will have to show that the gain is taxed in Spain. The Spaniards will tax your gains to Spanish income tax, which is usually worse than UK tax.

The UK/Spain double tax treaty rules under Article 13 for an individual who is resident in Spain are:

1 A capital gain from the disposal of *immovable property* situated in the UK is taxable in the UK. Immovable property includes land and also goods and plant involved in the use of the land, eg livestock, agricultural and forestry equipment etc. It also includes the enjoyment of land, mineral rights, fishing and/or shooting rights, etc, and extends to include property which is let.

2  A capital gain from *movable property* used in a place of business operation, in the UK, of either a Spanish resident or a Spanish business, is taxable in the UK. Examples of movable property are plant and machinery, fixtures and fittings, and other fixed assets of a UK business, and also goodwill.

3  Notwithstanding (2) above, a Spanish resident's capital gain from the disposal of a ship or aircraft operated in international traffic is taxable only in Spain.

4  Anything not mentioned above is taxable only in Spain.

## 9.14  Foreign currency: a note

Gains on foreign currency are liable to UK capital gains tax. This is so even if the currency is used to acquire other foreign investments or to buy a foreign property without any conversion into sterling. The Inland Revenue treat transfers between foreign currency bank accounts as one account, so that capital gains tax does not then arise (see Inland Revenue Statement of Practice SP10/84).

The tax treatment of foreign currency accounts is a trap for the unwary.

## 9.15  Payment dates of UK capital gains tax

The normal date of payments is 1 December after the end of the tax year in which the gain was made, or 30 days after the issue of the assessment, if later. Penalties can be charged if the capital gain is not reported to the Inland Revenue well before 1 December. Interest can be charged on late paid tax.

The tax can be paid by instalments where the proceeds of the sale are received by instalments over 18 months or more and paying the tax in one sum would cause hardship.

## 9.16  Capital gains tax on death

No capital gains tax charge arises on death – is this the ultimate tax plan? The Inland Revenue appear to have accepted the fact that death is not a tax planning 'technique'.

## 9.17  Hold-over relief and gifts

Hold-over relief avoids capital gains tax on gifts of business assets.

Gifts between husband and wife who are living together cannot give rise to a capital gains tax liability.

Usually any other gifts (including a sale at a low price to a relative or partner) will be liable to capital gains tax, and the Inland Revenue will substitute market price for the contract price. If the donor of business assets is an individual or trust, and the donee is an individual or trust who would be liable to capital gains tax on the subsequent disposal of the asset, by making an election in writing no capital gains tax is payable. This election is known as hold over relief. The donee's cost base for capital gains tax purposes is the price paid or the donor's original cost basis (whichever is higher). Business assets include shares in a family-owned company or property in a family business. Under the 1989 Budget Proposals, hold-over relief for non-business assets will no longer be given.

Where hold-over relief applies, if the donee becomes non-resident within six years after the end of the tax year in which the gift was made, the tax becomes payable. There is no such time limit for trustees, ie whenever the trust becomes non-resident, capital gains tax would be due. The election should be jointly made by donor and donee unless the donee is a trust in which case only the donor need claim.

Where part of the gain is covered by retirement relief, only the balance need be covered by the hold-over claim. If the gift attracts inheritance tax which is paid by the donee, the inheritance tax is added to the donee's base cost for future capital gains tax computations.

The hold-over relief can also be used for gifts of business assets from an individual to a company (but not vice versa). The claim can only be made if the gift is an asset used in the business, or shares in a 'family' company.

## 9.18 British forces overseas

If you work overseas in HM Armed Forces, your employment earnings are treated as if you remained in the UK. PAYE would therefore continue to apply. However, the normal rules of residence and ordinary residence still apply, and thus there are opportunities to save capital gains tax, income tax and inheritance tax.

## 9.19 Capital gains tax planning points

There are several important tax planning points which arise from this chapter.

1  You can avoid UK capital gains tax by selling an asset in the tax year after you have left the UK, when you become *both* not resident and not ordinarily resident.

2  The Spanish tax capital gains to income tax. If you realise your gain after leaving the UK, but before you officially take up residence in Spain, you will avoid both UK and Spanish taxes. There are other ways to avoid the Spanish tax. Advice must be taken to achieve this result.

3  If you sell shares in the UK tax year when you are resident in Spain, you are protected from UK tax under the double tax treaty. However, you may then be liable to Spanish tax.

4  If you use an asset in a trade in the UK, becoming not resident does not avoid UK capital gains tax. Instead, incorporate the business or rent the asset before selling, and you can avoid the capital gains tax.

5  If, for a husband and wife team, one is resident while the other is not resident (and not ordinarily resident), it may be possible to transfer all the assets to the non-resident before selling tax free. Professional advice should be taken to avoid some pitfalls.

6  Creative use of roll-over relief can save large amounts of capital gains tax (see sections 9.8 and 9.9).

7  Selling shares, and rolling over the gain into shares in a large public company (or loan stock of that company), avoids paying any capital gains tax. You should obtain clearance from the Inland Revenue in advance to obtain roll-over relief. The shares can then be sold (or the loan repaid) tax free when you leave the UK. The loan stock can have conversion rights to shares, if you so negotiate. If it is your known intention to avoid tax in this way, the Inland Revenue will not give you clearance.

*Chapter 10*

# Your UK Home

## 10.1 Letting your home: tax deductible costs

If you decide to continue to own your UK house, but to let it, you will continue to be liable for UK tax on the rental income even if you are not resident and not ordinarily resident in the UK. The UK includes England, Northern Ireland, Scotland and Wales.

The following costs can usually be deducted against the income:

general and water rates where paid by the landlord;
agent's fees;
legal fees relating to the letting (including VAT);
repairs and redecoration (see Section 10.2);
postage and telephone costs directly relating to the letting;
wear and tear (see Section 10.3);
other services (electricity, gas, TV/paid by the landlord);
insurance;
inventory fees;
ground rent;
valuation fees for insurance purposes;
gardening costs or window cleaning, if imposed on the landlord by the lease;
accountancy fees;
interest costs (see Section 10.4);
VAT charged (see Section 10.6).

### Rent receivable

The income is *not* the rent paid; it is the rent due under the terms of the lease in any tax year (6 April to 5 April). No adjustment is to be made for prepaid rent. The accounts must always be drawn up for the year to 5 April (although in practice the Inland Revenue do not always insist on this). Only if it can be shown that unpaid rent due is irrecoverable, after all reasonable steps have been taken to recover it, can the income be reduced to take account of unpaid rent.

## 10.2 Repairs and redecoration

Repairs and redecoration must be 'normal', ie outlay necessary to protect the property from dilapidations or to make good dilapidations which have already occurred. This cannot include expenditure on improvements, additions or alterations to the premises. The repairs and redecorations must be incurred and the work carried out when the tenant is in occupation, or between lettings, *not* before or after the tenancies. Furthermore, expenditure on making good dilapidations occurring before you acquired your interest in the property cannot qualify as repairs.

## 10.3 Wear and tear

An allowance for wear and tear on furniture, carpets, fittings etc may be claimed. If the letting is treated as a trade, the allowance is in the form of capital allowances, currently 25 per cent. However, the Inland Revenue scrutinise such claims closely and in most cases the letting is treated as unearned or investment income. It would be very unusual for a non-UK resident to be able to establish his lettings as a trade. There are two methods of allowance commonly approved by inspectors:

- 10 per cent of the net rental income (ie gross rents less rates and services) as a wear and tear allowance; or
- the net cost of replacements, but nothing for initial purchases.

## 10.4 Interest

Interest on a loan is deductible against the rental income if:

- the loan was used only to purchase or improve the property;
- the property is let at a commercial rent, not at a low rent to a friend or relative;
- it is let for at least 26 weeks in a 52-week period which includes the interest payment date and is either available for letting or under repair for the remainder of the period;
- in most cases, the interest is paid to a UK bank, not an overseas one; and
- the interest is payable on a loan not an overdraft.

If these conditions are met, there is *no limit* on the loan, unlike the

£30,000 limit applied to your home mortgage when you live there. However, relief for the interest can be given only against UK rental income. It cannot be claimed against any other UK income.

## 10.5 Tax deducted at source by tenant

If the tenant pays you the rent direct, he is required to deduct UK tax at 27 per cent on the gross rent and pay that to the Inland Revenue. If, on the other hand, a UK agent collects the rent, the tenant does not deduct tax. The agent is then responsible for any unpaid tax.

As the agent is responsible for the tax, he would normally ensure that a reserve was made out of your rental income in order to pay the Inland Revenue. If you use a relative as your agent, you should warn him that he will receive the tax assessments in his name. Where no agent exists, the Inland Revenue will enforce their collection rights upon the tenant even if he omits to deduct the income tax. It is not unusual for such a person to withhold future rent until his loss is made good. A good agent would know the likely tax payable and only reserve the minimum, paying you the balance.

## 10.6 Value added tax

Although you may live overseas, any invoices relating to the property (eg agents' fees, repairs, surveyors' fees, legal fees) have to carry VAT if the supplier is VAT registered. The VAT can be deducted as a cost in arriving at the taxable profit.

## 10.7 Income tax payment dates

There are two kinds of letting:

   unfurnished letting: taxable under Schedule A;
   furnished letting: taxable under Case VI of Schedule D.

*Unfurnished lettings* are usually taxed on the income of the *previous* tax year. Thus for the tax year 1988/89, the tax due is based on the income for the year to 5 April 1988. The tax is payable on 1 January 1989. The interest deducted is usually that paid in the tax year (ie year to 5 April 1989 in this example). Since the tax is payable before the interest is known, an estimate is usually made, and an adjustment made later.

*Furnished lettings* are taxed on the income of the *same* tax year, not the previous one. The tax is again payable on 1 January. Since the income will not be absolutely known at that time (as the tax year does not end until 5 April), an estimate of tax is made and adjusted later. Any tax deducted at source by the tenant or agent (see Section 10.5) is set off against the tax due (and might give rise to a refund).

### 10.8 UK capital gains tax: your own home

If you sell the property in a tax year in which you are both not resident and not ordinarily resident (these terms are defined in Sections 8.1 and 8.7), there is no UK capital gains tax due. If you are planning to return to the UK, and have a potential UK capital gains tax liability on your house, you may be better off selling it in the tax year *before* you return when you are not resident and not ordinarily resident. That way, you'll avoid UK capital gains tax.

*Provided a house has been your only or main residence at some time, the last two years of ownership are always exempt from capital gains tax.*

There are many other rules about avoiding capital gains tax on a principal private residence (your own home), which are rather complex but worth setting out in detail as this is often a key point for the working expatriate. Note that the rules for interest relief (MIRAS etc) and capital gains tax exemption are entirely separate.

### More than one residence

It must be borne in mind that you can have two residences available to you without owning them both. A home which you rent counts as a residence. An overseas flat or house – whether owned or rented – is also a residence.

If you own (or have available) more than one residence, you can elect which property should be regarded as the principal private residence for the capital gains tax exemption. Such an election, which must be in writing, cannot apply for a period starting earlier than two years prior to the election. The election can be varied at any time by giving a fresh notice, but again the variation cannot apply to any period over two years before the date of the new election. If no election is made, the Inspector of Taxes will choose, on the basis on what appears to him, on his examination of the facts, to be the main residence at the time. A second property which you let to bona fide tenants (or keep available for letting) is not treated as being available to you.

## Time limit for election
The Revenue consider that the time limit for making the election is two years from the date the second residence first becomes available. Most people doubt their interpretation of the legislation and in practice elections are often accepted outside this limit (but not so as to operate more than two years retrospectively). The Revenue have stated that where the taxpayer's interest in one of the properties has 'no more than a negligible capital value in the open market' and the taxpayer was unaware that an election could be made, they will extend the time limit to a reasonable time after the individual first becomes aware that he is entitled to make an election. They will then treat it as having effect from the date on which he acquired the second residence (Inland Revenue Extra-Statutory Concession D21). This concession is intended to cover the position where one of the properties is rented and the taxpayer did not realise that it constitutes a residence.

## Husband and wife
A husband and wife can only have one main residence between them while they are living together. Where a private residence election affects both (eg joint ownership) it must be given by both.

## The capital gains computation
If you let your house (or leave it unoccupied), and sell it in a tax year when you are resident (or ordinarily resident) in the UK, you may have a capital gains tax liability for the period let (or unoccupied). The amount of the gain which remains free of capital gains tax is:

$$\text{Total gain} \times \frac{\text{Number of weeks owned as principal private residence}}{\text{Number of weeks owned}}$$

Remember that the number of weeks which count as your owning it as a principal private residence always includes:

- the last 24 months, even if let;
- all weeks prior to 6 April 1965, even if let.

## Periods of absence
In the calculation above, certain periods of absence can also count as being periods when the house is your principal private residence, even though factually it was not (eg it can even be let).

These periods of absence are as follows.

- Any period (or periods) not exceeding three years; *plus*

- Any period where you worked overseas as an employee and all the duties were performed overseas. There is no time limit. Note that if the husband works but the wife does not, she would still be eligible for relief for her part ownership as long as she is living with the husband. This exemption does not apply if you are self-employed, nor does it apply if *any* of the duties were performed in the UK, however incidental they might be; *plus*
- Up to four years where your job in the UK requires you to live elsewhere (usually means more than 100 miles away).

There are several major traps in obtaining any of the above three periods of relief. You must meet each of the following three conditions:

- The house must be your main residence *before* the start of the period of absence; *and*
- It must be your main residence at some time *subsequent* to the period of absence. This means you must reoccupy the house before you sell it. There is no legal limit on the minimum time the house must be occupied, and some say that even one week is sufficient, so long as you have no other residence available. The Inland Revenue have stated that they believe the minimum period is three months, but their view has not been tested in the courts. There is one exception to having to reoccupy before you sell. The Inland Revenue have granted a concession where you are forced by your job to live elsewhere in the UK on your return; *and*
- You must have no other residence eligible for relief during the periods of absence. Of course, while overseas you are bound to have your overseas house available for your use as a residence. In practice the Inland Revenue tend to ignore this, though there is no guarantee that they will continue to adopt this approach. It is therefore *advisable* to submit a written election to the Inland Revenue within two years of going overseas that your UK home is to be treated as your principal private residence. If you do not make the election, the Inland Revenue could claim that your overseas home is your main residence, and hence you will fail to meet this condition.

### Separation or divorce
Where a married couple separate or are divorced and one partner (usually the husband) moves out and subsequently, as part of a financial settlement, disposes of the home (or his interest in it) to the

other, it can be regarded as continuing as the husband's main residence during the period up to the date of the transfer provided that it continues to be the wife's main residence throughout that period and the husband does not have another property which he is claiming to be his main residence (Inland Revenue Extra-Statutory Concession D6). It should particularly be noted that this applies only where the house is ultimately transferred to the wife. If it is sold and all or part of the proceeds paid to her the concession will not operate. In such a case it may be preferable to transfer the property to the wife and allow her to sell it.

### Buying while overseas
An expatriate who buys a UK house while he is overseas would not have met the rule of using the house both *before* and after a period of absence as his principal private residence. While there may be relief for interest purposes (see Section 10.11) there is no relief for capital gains tax purposes. Instead the expatriate should consider selling the house in the tax year *before* he returns, while he is both not resident and not ordinarily resident, when he is exempt from all capital gains tax (see Section 9.4). By concession, if you work full time overseas, the Revenue will regard you as both not resident and not ordinarily resident until the day you return to the UK, in which case it would appear unnecessary to sell the house in the tax year before you return; selling before you return, even in the same tax year, would be sufficient. However, if possible you should not rely too heavily on this concession as it can always be withdrawn.

### Avoiding capital gains tax *and* keeping the house
As an alternative to selling in the tax year before return to the UK to a third party, you could transfer it to a trust for yourself and your wife's benefit. The transfer into the trust will be tax free if the requirements of not resident and not ordinarily resident are met, and any subsequent disposal by the trust will also be tax free if the property is occupied by you under the terms of the trust.

### 10.9 'Available' accommodation

A house which is commercially let will not be treated as 'available' accommodation for the purposes of determining UK residence status.

## 10.10 Losses?

A loss figure can be carried forward to be set against rents of a similar nature in future years.

## 10.11 Working abroad and MIRAS

Keeping a house in the UK will not in itself affect your UK tax residence status. You may still even be able to continue with your MIRAS (*Mortgage Interest Relief At Source*).

Since 6 April 1983 (or in some cases even earlier) mortgage interest on house loans may be paid after deduction of tax at the basic rate, for the income tax year in which the payment becomes due, if the interest is 'relevant loan interest' paid by you being a 'qualifying borrower' to a 'qualifying lender'.

1 'Relevant loan interest' is interest paid and payable in the UK to a 'qualifying lender' and it is interest on loans for the purchase of a residence including a residential caravan or houseboat in the UK which when the interest is paid is used wholly, or to a substantial extent, as the only or main residence of the borrower. Before 5 April 1988 relief was also available for the purchase of a residence for a dependent relative or separated or former spouse and for home improvements. Interest relief will continue for such loans until they are repaid *or* replaced.

2 'Qualifying borrower' is any individual who pays 'relevant loan interest'. There is an exception to this. If you or your husband or wife receive(s) earnings that are exempt from UK tax, eg certain Crown and Foreign Office appointments, neither of you can qualify for MIRAS. There are very few tax exempt occupations.

3 A 'qualifying lender' includes a building society, a local authority, the Bank of England, an insurance company authorised to carry on long-term business (eg life assurance) in the UK, a trustee savings bank, an existing lender under the mortgage option scheme, and any recognised bank or licensed deposit-taking institution authorised by the Treasury.

MIRAS enables you to reduce your mortgage interest payments by the basic rate of tax (25 per cent, post 1988 Budget). It is limited to interest on the first £30,000 of a loan to buy your principal private residence. Even though you, as an expatriate, are no longer living in the UK and may have no UK income, you can still obtain MIRAS relief because of an Inland Revenue concession.

Where you are required by reason of your employment to move from your home to another place, either in the UK or abroad, for a period not expected to exceed four years, any property being bought with the aid of a mortgage, which was being used as your only or main residence *before* you went away, will still be treated as such, provided that it can reasonably be expected to be so again on your return. It is *not* sufficient to claim the first four years of an expected five-year absence. The maximum period is four years, but if there is a further temporary absence *after* the property has been reoccupied for a minimum period of three months, the four-year test will apply to the year of absence *without* regard to the previous absence.

If you are already working abroad and buy a property in the UK in the course of a leave period *and* use that property as an only or main residence for a period of not less than three months *before* your return to the place of your overseas employment, you will be regarded as satisfying the condition that the property was used as your only or main residence before you went away.

If you let your property at a commercial rent while you are away, the benefit of the concession may be claimed where appropriate, if this is more favourable than a claim for relief against letting income.

If you go abroad but leave your family in your UK house, MIRAS relief will not be subject to the above-mentioned four-year time limit.

## 10.12 The building society

Under the terms of your mortgage, you will no doubt discover that you are obliged to inform your building society if you no longer personally occupy your house. If you tell them that you intend to let the property, the building society may refuse their permission. They might agree if you are only leaving the UK for less than three years, have paid all your mortgage payments on time, and agree to pay a higher interest rate. They will probably want to review the tenancy agreement and they would insist that:

- no tenant enjoying diplomatic immunity be accepted (this is because you cannot sue such a tenant, or get him out of your house);
- the tenancy agreement must not allow the tenant to sublet or part with possession of any part of the property, either with or without your consent;

143

- the rent agreed must be paid either weekly or monthly;
- the rent must be sufficient to cover all outgoings;
- you serve a valid notice on the proposed tenant under Case 11 of the 1977 Rent Act (1984 Rent Act in Scotland; 1978 Rent Order in Northern Ireland). This gives you more rights as a person intending to return to your own home in the UK. There are special Rent Act provisions for members of the Armed Forces.

The permission – if granted – may only be for a period of three years, with your having to reapply at the end of the three years.

## 10.13 Insurers

You must inform your insurers that you intend to let the house, otherwise the policy may be void. An extra premium may be payable. They may insist that if the house is empty for any period of more than 24 hours, the cold water tank be drained. You must read the small print carefully. The policy will only pay out on theft if there are signs of forcible entry. You will not be covered for theft by your tenant unless you take out a policy which covers larceny.

## 10.14 The lease to the tenant

It is advisable to have a solicitor deal with your lease. There are ways to safeguard your position.

One way is to draw up a 'short-hold' tenancy agreement under the 1980 Housing Act. This will give you the right to re-entry to your home on the expiry of the agreement, provided you have complied with the provisions of the Act. These agreements can be for a period of between one and five years.

A second way is to give a 'Case 11 notice' which is a notice stating to the tenant before the lease is signed that you are an owner-occupier within the meaning of the 1977 Rent Act, and you will require possession for personal occupation at the end of the lease. The tenant must acknowledge receipt of this notice. The minimum notice period is four weeks, or the period for which rent is collected if greater. If on your return you cannot physically occupy the premises because you are required to work elsewhere in the UK by your employer, you can still obtain possession.

A third way is to let the property to a company, since a company has fewer rights. It is possible for a company to create a 'rent legislation protected' tenancy, so your agreement must contain a covenant restricting the company from creating such a 'protected' tenancy. Considerable difficulty can be experienced if you do not use a competent solicitor in drawing up the agreement.

## 10.15 Sheltering the rental income from UK tax

There is no limit to interest deductibility on loans used to purchase or improve a property which is commercially let. If you are buying a property, you should use as little of your own money as possible.

### Example

If you were intending to invest, say, £250,000 of your own money and take out a mortgage of £50,000, you may be arranging your affairs in the wrong way. Instead, consider taking out a mortgage of 70 per cent (£200,000, say), using only £100,000 of your money rather than £250,000. The remaining £150,000 can be invested tax free outside the UK. You should not overdo this: the Revenue tend to attack loans in excess of 70 per cent of the purchase price.

As long as your loans meet the conditions set out in section 10.4, you can now:

- Deduct interest on £350,000 of loans against rental income, not £200,000. This will reduce your UK tax bill.
- Invest £150,000 overseas with the opportunity of having it invested in a tax haven in a tax sheltered form.

## 10.16 Appointing an accountant in the UK

It is well worth appointing on accountant who is experienced in lettings and capital gains tax to ensure that you minimise your tax liability. In addition, the accountant can take the responsibility of dealing with the Inland Revenue, and minimising the amount of tax deducted at source by your agent. He can also receive all tax assessments direct from your Inspector of Taxes, ensure appropriate appeals are made within the 30-day limit which can be difficult to meet from overseas, and he can prepare your annual UK tax return.

## 10.17 The poll tax

The poll tax (Community Charge) started in Scotland on 1 April 1989 and comes into operation in England and Waless on 1 April 1990, and is not an April Fool's joke. It replaces domestic rates. There are a number of exempt individuals, and full-time students need only pay 20 per cent of the total charge. The charge will vary enormously depending on the local authority. A Camden resident can expect a bill of £600 per adult while if you live in Croydon it will be about £200 per adult, but these figures have still to be confirmed.

The charge is payable on any unoccupied property by the owner, unless it is let on a lease for more than six months, in which case the tenant is liable. For people with second homes in the UK, the local authority can charge up to twice the usual charge. Anyone over the age of 18 (including live-in staff such as nannies) must register, and pay the tax.

## 10.18 UK house tax and financial planning

### Expenses
If you rent your house, ensure that you claim as many expenses as you can, including repairs, redecoration, telephone costs, gardener, wear and tear, accountancy costs.

### Interest unlimited
When you rent your house, the £30,000 loan limit does *not* apply. You can claim interest on an *unlimited* loan, as long as it meets certain requirements, ie it is a loan (not an overdraft) from a UK bank and was only used to purchase or improve the property. However, part of the interest may be disallowed if the loan is in excess of usual commercial terms (thus 70 per cent of the valuation of the property is a normal commercial loan limit).

### Repairs and redecoration
Avoid carrying out any repairs or redecoration either before you first let the house or just after you have permanently stopped letting, as the costs will not be deductible. Only redecorate between lettings (or while the tenant is in occupation).

### Avoid capital gains tax
There are many ways to avoid capital gains tax, yet numerous pitfalls for the unwary. Read Section 8.8 carefully. In particular, you

ought to make an election, in writing, within two years of leaving the UK, that your UK house is to be regarded as your principal private residence.

# Chapter 11

# UK Income Tax

## 11.1 Introduction

UK income tax is always payable on income arising in the UK, but is not payable on any other income as long as the taxpayer is not resident in the UK (see Sections 8.1 and 8.2). Reduced rates of tax may be payable under the operation of the double tax treaty. A useful book is IR 20, *Residents' and Non-Residents' Tax Liability in the United Kingdom* available from any Inland Revenue office.

## 11.2 UK rates of tax

The current rates are:

|  | 1989–90 | 1988–89 |
|---|---|---|
| Basic rate | 25% | 25% |
| Basic rate band up to | £20,700 | £19,300 |
| Maximum basic rate tax | £5,175 | £4,825 |
| Higher rate | 40% | 40% |

## 11.3 UK personal allowances

The main personal allowances are:

|  | 1989–90 | 1988–89 |
|---|---|---|
| Single personal and wife's earnings | £2,785 | £2,605 |
| Married personal | £4,375 | £4,095 |
| Single parent families, widows etc | £1,590 | £1,490 |
| Maintenance payments relief – maximum | £1,590 | £1,490 |
| Age relief – single person | £3,400 | £3,180 |
| – married couple | £5,385 | £5,035 |
| Higher age relief – single person | £3,540 | £3,310 |
| – married couple | £5,565 | £5,205 |
| Age limit for higher age relief | 75yrs | 80yrs |

| | | |
|---|---|---|
| Age relief reduced for income over | £11,400 | £10,600 |
| Age relief reduced by | ½ | ⅔ |
| Wife's earnings election minimum joint income | £30,511 | £28,484 |
| Business Expansion Scheme relief | £40,000 | £40,000 |

A non-resident may claim personal allowance on what is effectively a proportionate basis. For example, if a married man has £10,000 of UK income and £20,000 of overseas income (total worldwide income being £30,000), he would be entitled to one-third of the £4,375 married person's allowance.

Claiming this allowance will generate a tax saving of £1,094 if he pays UK tax at 25 per cent and more if his UK income brings him into the higher rates of tax.

This tax saving can be improved following a case brought against the Inland Revenue in 1984 by a man called Addison. Where the overseas investment income belongs to the non-resident's wife, it can be left out of account altogether.

There is no restriction similar to this for personal allowances on allowable loan interest or on the benefit of the higher rate tax bands.

It is important to note that the overseas income is not itself taxed. It is merely taken into account to determine what tax is payable on any UK income. None the less, because many taxpayers are reluctant to disclose this information to the UK Inland Revenue, this allowance is often not claimed. If the Revenue are aware of the extent of your overseas income, this may make it more difficult to convince them that you have changed your residence or domicile status.

This restriction over the personal allowance is often thought to be unfair, especially for those who have retired on a government pension. Their pension is fully liable to UK tax – wherever they live – but their personal allowance can be restricted if they have overseas income. One way around this is to let the wife have all the overseas income, and follow the path trodden by Mr Addison mentioned above.

Many people have not bothered to claim the personal allowances because it has meant declaring their worldwide income to the UK authorities, and since the allowance is often so derisory the effort is not worth while. Since 6 April 1989 this has changed, and expatriates are now able to obtain a much larger tax allowance. The changes are:

1 There will be no restriction on claiming personal allowances, and thus no need to declare your worldwide income.

2 Both husband and wife will be eligible for the allowance, and can each make a separate claim.

If an expatriate has a UK bank deposit account or 'non-resident' UK building society account, the interest is tax free by virtue of an extra-statutory concession known as B3. However, such interest is taken into account when personal allowances are claimed in the UK against UK income. It is advisable to keep such deposit accounts outside the UK (eg in the Channel Islands) to avoid UK tax.

## 11.4  UK pensions

UK pensions paid to a non-resident are liable to UK tax unless the pensioner is exempted by a double tax agreement or the pension is paid out under one of the following schemes:

- India, Pakistan, Burma and Colonial schemes
- Pension funds for former public service employees of overseas territories
- The Central African Pension Fund
- The Overseas Service Pension Fund
- Pension funds set up for overseas employees of UK employers.

The UK/Spanish double taxation agreement taxes pensions only in Spain if you are resident there, with the exception of pensions paid out of public funds in the UK, which *remain* taxable in the UK. 'Public funds' includes pensions paid to former servants of the Crown, and pensions paid for services rendered to a local authority in the UK. Such public fund pensions may be free of UK tax under the double taxation agreement if the pensioner is a national of Spain.

If your pension is going to be liable for UK income tax or Spanish tax, it may be better to elect to take a tax-free lump sum and to reduce the level of pension liable to tax.

UK social security pensions are payable in Spain including cost of living increases though these will be related to the British cost of living index. There is a leaflet, SA29, produced by the DSS which discusses this.

## 11.5  UK rental income

This is taxable in full in the UK even if you are not resident as it 'arises' in the UK. Rental income arising from your own house is discussed in Chapter 10. Interest to a UK bank (not a foreign one) is deductible if it complies with the conditions set out in Section 10.4. The tax is payable in the UK according to the rules set out in Section 10.5.

## 11.6 UK dividends

Dividends from UK companies constitute taxable income. However, they carry with them a tax credit which covers the shareholder's liability to basic rate tax. For example, a £100 dividend can be expressed as follows:

| Dividend | Tax credit |
|----------|------------|
| £100 | £33.33 |

The figures used are for the 1989/90 UK tax year, and the tax credit is 25 per cent of the aggregate sum. This 25 per cent tax rate is the basic rate of tax in the UK.

Under the UK/Spain double taxation agreement, it is possible to claim a refund or part of the tax credit. The refund amounts to 10 per cent of the dividend plus tax credit, leaving a 15 per cent effective UK tax rate. Credit is given in Spain for the 15 per cent tax paid in the UK.

If you control 10 per cent of the company (either directly or indirectly), the tax refund is increased to 15 per cent leaving only a 10 per cent UK tax rate.

It is possible for a UK company to enter into an arrangement with the UK Inspector of Foreign Dividends in effect to pay the tax refund to non-resident shareholders covered by the double tax agreement without their needing to make a formal claim. Many companies are unwilling to take on the increased administration and the liability to pay the Revenue any tax refunded to which it is subsequently discovered that the shareholder was not entitled.

## 11.7 UK Lloyd's earnings

Such earnings are liable to UK tax. Many offshore individuals reduce their UK tax exposure by giving a bank guarantee (secured by offshore assets) rather than depositing assets with Lloyd's (which increases the UK taxable income).

## 11.8 UK interest (banks and building societies)

Normal on-shore building society and bank accounts are not suitable for UK expatriates. Many societies and banks advertise 'international accounts' suggesting that payments may be made gross without risk of UK income tax. At first sight, these appear highly attractive when compared to the returns available on the high interest money market bank accounts. In theory such income is liable to UK tax but, by concession, the Inland Revenue often do not charge such tax if you are non-resident for the entire tax year and do not claim a tax repayment in respect of any other UK income that has suffered tax by deduction at source. Where other UK income arises in the UK, the tax may be easier to collect. For example, where a non-resident is in receipt of a government pension, there may be less reluctance on the part of the Inland Revenue to apply the concession. Many building society depositors who are living outside the UK have found that an assessment has been raised in these circumstances. This assessment may be dropped where the depositor can provide evidence that the income has been declared in his new country of residence (eg, Spain). If the interest is taxed in Spain, the UK tax rate is reduced to 12 per cent (with tax credit given in Spain).

In addition, if the non-resident is not domiciled in the UK, he would be putting his capital at risk unnecessarily to a charge to inheritance tax. Finally, interest in the UK suffers from tax deducted at source (called composite rate tax) and it is thus always preferable for a non-resident to invest in gross funds outside the UK.

## 11.9 UK gilts

Gilts are publicly quoted stocks backed fully by the British government. At no time has a British government failed to meet any of its funded debt obligations whether in the nature of capital or income, but don't be fooled into thinking that gilts are always safe. If you have to sell before maturity, you can lose a lot of money. How much you lose or gain depends on what has happened to interest rates.

When you buy a gilt, you are lending the government money at a guaranteed interest rate (called the 'coupon'). Repayment is normally due at a specified date, so you can work out exactly how much you will receive, and when, although the government have the right to repay some stocks at any time over a three- to five-year period. Rates of return are often higher than from a bank or building society, and the guarantee is stronger – the government is less likely to go bankrupt than Barclays Bank or Abbey National.

## UK tax position

Interest on gilts is liable to UK income tax and the majority have tax deducted at source. However, there are a number of gilts on which there is no tax due either on income or capital gain if you are not resident in the UK. It will be up to you to prove your non-resident status though; it is not enough simply to provide a foreign address; you may have to give details of your tax reference number and district in Spain. In order to get approval, you should obtain Form A3 from the Inspector of Foreign Dividends, Lynwood Road, Thames Ditton, Surrey KT7 0DP. Unless you have already been cleared as non-resident, expect some searching questions about your long-term plans, duration of visits, location of home, and so on.

The list of gilt stocks which are free of tax to residents abroad may be obtained from the Bank of England, Threadneedle Street, London, EC1. These are specifically designed for non-residents and pay gross interest from the outset, subject to satisfactory evidence of non-resident status.

The list of such stocks at 12 August 1988 is:

| | | | |
|---|---|---|---|
| 9% | Conversion Stock 2000 | 5½% | Treasury Stock 2008/12 |
| 9% | Conversion Stock 2011 | 6¾% | Treasury Stock 1995/98 |
| 9½% | Conversion Stock 2001 | 7¾% | Treasury Stock 2012/15 |
| 9¾% | Conversion Stock 2003 | 8% | Treasury Convertible Stock 1990 |
| 11% | Exchequer Stock 1990 | 8% | Treasury Loan 1992 |
| 13¼% | Exchequer Stock 1996 | 8% | Treasury Stock 2002/06 |
| 5¾% | Funding Stock 1987/91 | 8¼% | Treasury Stock 1987/90 |
| 6% | Funding Stock 1993 | 8½% | Treasury Stock 2000 |
| 2% | Index-linked Treasury Stock 1992 | 8½% | Treasury Stock 2007 |
| 2½% | Index-linked Treasury Stock 2024 | 8¾% | Treasury Stock 1997 |
| 9% | Treasury Stock 1992/96 | 12¾% | Treasury Stock 1992 |
| 9% | Treasury Stock 1994 | 12¾% | Treasury Stock 1995 |
| 9% | Treasury Stock 2008 | 13% | Treasury Stock 1990 |
| 9½% | Treasury Stock 1999 | 13¼% | Treasury Stock 1997 |
| 10% | Treasury Convertible Stock 1991 | 3¾% | Treasury Stock 1993 |
| 10% | Treasury Stock 1993 | 14½% | Treasury Stock 1994 |
| 10% | Treasury Stock 1994 | 15¼% | Treasury Stock 1996 |
| 10½% | Treasury Convertible Stock 1992 | 15½% | Treasury Stock 1998 |
| 12½% | Treasury Stock 1993 | 3½% | War Stock |

**Advantages**

Gilts are a good investment to meet a future known liability or to obtain a fixed return on capital. They can be useful as part of a portfolio, especially where it is felt that interest rates will fall. Index-linked gilts and low-coupon gilts favour higher rate taxpayers.

**Disadvantages**

Small investors have avoided gilts for several reasons. First, they appear complicated. Gilts come in different shapes and sizes. They differ in prices, rates of return and maturity dates. Second, they are avoided because of inflation. In 1945–80 gilts were a poor investment. Indeed, the real rate of return has sometimes been negative, as inflation rates have far exceeded the interest rates earned. This is true of any fixed rate investment, including bank and building society deposits. Third, gilts can lose you money if you sell them before maturity and interest rates have risen since you purchased your stock.

There are a number of extremely successful high income producing offshore funds investing exclusively in UK government stock. This will provide far more active, and generally more successful, management than holding stock direct. Where gilts are required to provide for capital growth as opposed to income, there are specific low coupon, short-dated, British government stock unit trusts available within the UK which have certain advantages for offshore investors.

## 11.10 UK royalties

Under the double taxation treaty, the maximum UK tax payable is 10 per cent.

## 11.11 UK employment earnings

These are taxable in the UK assuming the employment is undertaken in the UK. It is, however, only taxable in Spain, and not the UK, if:

- You are resident in Spain
- You spend less than 182 days in a tax year in the UK
- The salary is paid by a non-UK employer
- The salary is not borne by a permanent establishment or a fixed base of the employer in the UK.

Where you work for a UK employer, full UK tax would be payable.

There are special rules for artists, entertainers, students, teachers and government service.

## 11.12 Obtaining a tax refund in year of leaving UK

A refund of income tax may arise in the year of leaving the UK where the taxpayer has suffered PAYE. The PAYE system spreads the annual personal allowances over the full year, but you are entitled to the full personal allowances even if you leave part-way through a tax year. Thus you may have paid too much PAYE and by completing the form P85 (see Section 8.5) you can apply for a refund.

## 11.13 Maintenance or alimony

There are two kinds of payment: voluntary or legally binding.

### Voluntary
Payments between a husband and wife under voluntary arrangements have no tax effect.

### Legally binding in the UK
The 1988 Finance Act introduced substantial changes for new court orders or new agreements. Maintenance payments have been virtually removed from the UK tax system.

Any recipient of maintenance will not be taxable on maintenance. This applies to children as well as wives.

The payer can only obtain tax relief for up to £1590 per annum against UK taxable income if the payments are payments of maintenance to a spouse which are legally binding *in the UK* (not those only legally binding in Spain), ie the payments are made under a UK court order or an agreement made under UK law. No relief is available at all for payments to children of the marriage even if no maintenance is paid to the wife. The payer cannot obtain relief for payments to the extent that they exceed £1590, and this relief will stop if the payer remarries, even if the maintenance payments continue. Transitional tax relief is given for agreements or court orders entered into before the new rules take effect.

### Husband and wife
As explained in Section 8.1, husband and wife are treated separately.

Thus it is possible for the husband to be UK non-resident while his wife remains resident; see Sections 8.1 and 8.2 for more details.

## 11.4 UK income tax planning points

1 Generally speaking, income arising in the UK is liable to UK income tax, even though in some cases a reduced rate of tax is payable. The simplest way to avoid UK income tax is to arrange your affairs to avoid any income arising in the UK.
2 You can increase your UK allowances by transferring investment income to your wife. This is the Addison case described in Section 11.3.
3 Complete your form P85 before you leave the UK to obtain your tax refund. Take professional advice in completing it, however.
4 It may suit you if your wife (or husband) was not resident in the UK, while you remain resident. The residence status in the UK is determined independently.

# Chapter 12

# UK Inheritance Tax

## 12.1 Introduction

Inheritance tax liabilities have nothing to do with whether or not you are resident or ordinarily resident in the UK. Instead, UK inheritance tax (which we shall call IHT) is based on your *domicile*.

Domicile is explained in Section 12.10. It is something like nationality. If you are domiciled in the UK, then no matter where you live you are liable for IHT on your worldwide assets, *including all your assets in Spain or elsewhere.*

It is extremely difficult to change your domicile. If you are not domiciled in the UK, but in (say) Spain, you are still liable to IHT but only on assets located in the UK.

## 12.2 Rates of tax

IHT bites quickly and hard. It is not only a tax for the very rich, as quite modest estates are liable to the tax.

**1988/89 Rates**

*Cumulative chargeable*

| Gross transfers | Rate |
|---|---|
| £ | % |
| 1–118,000 | nil |
| over 118,000 | 40 |

Thus the tax on a £500,000 estate is £152,800.

## 12.3 IHT basic rules

IHT is chargeable where there is a 'transfer of value'. A transfer of value is defined as any disposition which reduces the value of your estate with the intention of conferring a gratuitous benefit. For simplicity, we will refer to this as 'gifts'.

## 1 Death
Tax is chargeable on the whole of the estate, unless it is exempt (eg between husband and wife).

## 2 Lifetime gifts
A gift is chargeable, unless it is exempt. The amount chargeable is the reduction in value of the estate as a result of the gift.

## 3 Exempt transfers
There are a variety of exempt gifts and these are listed in Section 12.4.

## 4 Potentially exempt transfers (PET)
Unlimited gifts made by an individual to:

(a) another individual; or
(b) an 'accumulation and maintenance settlement trust' (explained in Section 12.16); or
(c) a trust for disabled persons; or
(d) a trust in which another person has an 'interest in possession' (explained in Section 12.14)

and are all potentially exempt from IHT. This means that there is no IHT to pay as long as you survive for seven years after making the gift.

If you die within the seven years, the tax payable is reduced as follows:

| Years between gift and death | Full charge % |
|---|---|
| 0–3 | 100 |
| 3–4 | 80 |
| 4–5 | 60 |
| 5–6 | 40 |
| 6–7 | 20 |

and the 'full charge' is 50 per cent of the rates payable on death.

Note that even if you die within seven years, the growth in value of the assets given away is free of IHT. It is only the value of the gift when made which is taxable, not the value at date of death.

## 12.4 Exempt gifts

The following gifts are completely free of IHT from the time the transfer is made, and hence exemption does *not* rely on the donor surviving seven years.

### 1 Husband and wife
All gifts between husband and wife, unless the donor spouse is domiciled in the UK and the donee spouse is not UK domiciled, in which case IHT can be payable on anything in excess of £59,000.

### 2 Charities
All gifts to charities are free of IHT.

### 3 Annual
£3000 per annum can be given away (both husband and wife have a £3000 exemption). If any part is not used, it can be carried forward for up to one year, though the second year's exemption must be used before the carried forward allowance.

### 4 Normal income expenditure
Gifts forming part of normal (ie habitual) expenditure, and made out of income not needed to maintain the donor's standard of living, are free of IHT. It must be shown that taking one year with another and, that after allowing for the gift, the donor had sufficient income to maintain his standard of living. This can represent as much as 50 per cent of income. This exemption would normally cover payments under deeds of covenant or life assurance premiums where the policy is written in trust.

### 5 Marriage
Gifts in consideration of marriage are exempt up to:

   (a)  £5000 by *each* parent;
   (b)  £2500 by each grandparent (or other ancestor); and
   (c)  £1000 by anyone else.

Note that the gift must clearly be made in consideration of the marriage and for no other reason.

### 6 Maintenance
Lifetime gifts to maintain your own child or former spouse or reasonable provision for dependent relatives are free of IHT. Gifts to children which are exempt must be for the maintenance, education

or training of the child. A child includes a stepchild, adopted child or illegitimate child.

## 7 Waiver of remuneration or dividends

A waiver of remuneration is not a gift. A waiver of a dividend, made within 12 months of the right to the dividend, is not a gift.

## 8 Other

Other tax free gifts are:

- (a) for national purposes (eg National Gallery, British Museum, National Trust, universities);
- (b) political parties: unlimited, unless made within 12 months of death, in which case it is limited to £100,000; and
- (c) heritage property, eg outstanding historic buildings, some non-profit making trusts, various Treasury approved non-profit making bodies.

## 12.5 Husband and wife

Husband and wife are treated separately for IHT, unlike most other taxes. Thus each is separately eligible for the allowances (eg £118,000 limit), and gifts are not aggregated. There is one exception: if the Inland Revenue can prove 'associated operations', husband and wife may be treated as one. Professional advice should be sought.

## 12.6 The cumulation principle and IHT rates

A running total of chargeable lifetime gifts is kept and tax is only payable when the threshold (currently £118,000) is met. Both husband and wife each have their own threshold of £118,000. The tax rates then increase progressively through various bands. Gifts are dropped out of the running total after seven years from the date they are made. When someone dies, the tax payable is computed by valuing the estate and adding to it all gifts within seven years of death. Similarly, any tax payable on a lifetime gift is calculated by adding that gift to all gifts within seven years, and applying the tax rate to that latest one.

The rates of tax payable vary as follows.

## 1 Potentially exempt transfers (PETs)

A gift from an individual to another individual, or certain trust, is potentially free of IHT if the donor survives for seven years.

If the donor dies within three years, the full rate of tax is then payable. Between three and seven years, the rate of tax is reduced as follows:

| Years | % |
|-------|-----|
| 0–3 | 100 |
| 3–4 | 80 |
| 4–5 | 60 |
| 5–6 | 40 |
| 6–7 | 20 |

## 2 Other lifetime gifts

Any gift not potentially exempt is chargeable at 50 per cent of the full rates.

## 12.7 The seven-year rule

Seven-year survivorship is important for three reasons:

- potentially exempt gifts become free of IHT after seven years;
- chargeable lifetime gifts are excluded from the running total after seven years; and
- the tax on other lifetime gifts (which are chargeable at 50 per cent of the full rates) is recalculated if death occurs within seven years, and increased tax is payable.

## 12.8 Gifts with reservation

If you give away something, but reserve some benefit (eg, you give away your house, but continue living in it rent free), the entire property is treated as *remaining* in your estate. This happens even if the 'benefit' reserved is quite small. Thus a gift must be made outright and completely. If the reservation of benefit ends, it is treated as a gift from that date.

The sorts of 'gift' this rule is intended to catch are:

- gift of house which donor continues to occupy;
- gift of shares where donor continues to receive income; and
- gift into trust where the donor is (or can become) a beneficiary.

These rules include not only any benefit reserved at the time of the gift, but also any benefit which might arise later.

If the benefit reserved is removed, seven years may have to elapse before the transfer is free of IHT. If it is not removed, it will be treated as part of the donor's estate on his death. If the donor dies within seven years of the removal of the benefit (and after three years) reduced rates are payable.


## 12.9 Gifts of property with reservation

This area is full of pitfalls, and professional advice must be taken.

If property is given away, and full market rent is paid by the donor to continue in residence, this is *not* treated as a gift with reservation.

Alternatively, if the donor's occupation of the property arises because:

- the donor's circumstances change in an unforeseen way;
- the donor cannot maintain himself because of old age or infirmity;
- the property represents a reasonable provision by the donee for the care and maintenance of the donor; and
- the gift is by a donee who is the donor's relative or spouse's relative;

IHT will *not* arise.


## 12.10 UK domicile

**Introduction**
If you are domiciled in the UK, you (and your estate) remain liable for UK inheritance tax even though you may cease to be a UK resident and ordinarily resident.

You are domiciled in the country which you regard as your homeland – often described as the place where you 'belong'. You can only be domiciled in one place at a particular point of time, unlike residence where you can be resident in two countries simultaneously.

Your place of domicile does not have to be the country with which you have your closest personal association. A person can live in a country for many years and still remain domiciled elsewhere. It is very difficult to establish a change of domicile.

A person has a *domicile of origin*, which is normally the domicile of his father at the time of that person's birth. If your father's domicile changed before you reached age 16, you will have acquired his new domicile. A woman married prior to 1 January 1974 automatically acquired her husband's domicile – effectively as a domicile of choice.

The domicile of origin can be altered to become another country, called the *domicile of choice*. However, this is not easy. If you lose your domicile of choice, eg by leaving your adopted country and moving to a third country, you automatically re-acquire your domicile of origin. It is not necessary to change your nationality to acquire a new domicile, though obviously this could be a persuasive factor. The sort of things that the Revenue look at to consider where a person is domiciled is the country of which an individual has a passport, driving licence, or in which he has made a will, has arranged to be buried, is a club member, owns credit cards, personal insurances, bank accounts, and property, and has family.

Even if you manage to alter your domicile, you will avoid UK inheritance taxes only if you have no assets located in the UK. Non-UK domiciled persons are liable to UK inheritance tax on all assets located in the UK, even if they've never visited the UK! Ownership of such assets through a non-UK company will insulate them from this tax.

## Changing your domicile
Even changing your domicile and moving all your assets outside the UK is not quite enough. Changing your domicile can be ineffective if you have a *deemed UK domicile*. This concept applies only for inheritance tax purposes. You are deemed to be domiciled in the UK if:

- at any time *in the three calendar years prior* to an 'event' (ie gift or death), you were actually UK domiciled. In other words, UK domicile for inheritance tax purposes persists for three years *after* the acquisition of a new domicile; or
- you have been *resident in the UK for 17 of the 20 consecutive tax years* ending with the tax year in which there is an 'event' (gift or death). Residence has the same meaning as described earlier except that the existence of 'available' accommodation can be ignored.

The UK/Spain double tax treaty does not cover inheritance tax – the estate of a UK domiciled Spanish resident can end up paying two lots of inheritance tax, one in Spain, and one in the UK. Where this happens, the UK will normally grant a credit for the overseas tax paid, so you will end up paying tax at the higher of the UK or the Spanish tax rates.

## 12.11 Agricultural property relief

In valuing 'agricultural property' for IHT, a reduction is given of:

- 50 per cent if the land has vacant possession (or the right to vacant possession within 12 months); or
- 30 per cent if the land is tenanted.

'Agricultural property' includes:

agricultural land or pasture;
any building used for intensive rearing of livestock or fish;
ancillary buildings, including cottages, farm-houses, farm buildings; and
land or buildings connected with breeding or rearing of horses.

Agricultural property includes property in the Channel Islands or the Isle of Man.

The IHT reduction is only set against the agricultural value, not against any excess development value. The excess may attract relief as business property.

To qualify for relief, the property must have been either:

- *owned and occupied* by the donor for agricultural purposes throughout the two years ending on the date of the gift; or
- *owned* by the donor or throughout the previous seven years and occupied for agricultural purposes.

Where business property relief is due (see Section 12.12), agricultural property relief is given first.

Agricultural property relief can also be given against shares in a farming company where various conditions are met.

The relief is lost if the property is subject to a binding contract for sale when given away.

## 12.12 Business property relief

You do not have to be a business person to obtain business property relief. You have to own a certain type of property, and most businesses qualify.

The relief is given as a reduction in valuation for IHT purposes. The reductions are:

*50% for* a sole trader or partner's interest;
shares in *unquoted* companies in excess of 25 per cent of the voting power

shares in *quoted* companies in excess of 50 per cent of the voting power.

*30% for* any other *unquoted* shares, land or buildings, machinery or plant, used for the purposes of a business carried on by a company controlled by the transferor, by a partnership in which he was a partner or where it is owned by a trust in which the transferor has an interest in possession.

Where property is mortgaged, the relief is restricted to the net value of the property after deducting the loan.

### Ownership qualifications
To qualify for relief, the donor must have owned the property throughout the two years preceding the gift. The property must not be subject to a binding contract of sale at the time the gift is made.

No relief is available for shares in an investment company. Shares in a company whose trade consists of dealing in property, or shares, do not qualify.

### A trap
You will not obtain business property relief if there is a written agreement providing the shares to be sold (for example, to your other shareholders). However, there are ways of achieving the same result by the careful use of options, and professional advice should be taken.

## 12.13  Woodlands and Lloyd's underwriters

Special rules apply, and advice should be sought.

## 12.14  Trusts: introduction and definitions

### Introduction
Trusts are not only for the rich. Even if you are just comfortably off, one type of trust – the accumulation and maintenance trust – can be worth considering for your children, grandchildren or other infants, and many people who are not rich at all set up trusts in their wills. Additionally, you might leave all your capital in a trust so that on your death the income goes to your spouse, but on your spouse's death the capital is then divided among your children.

You may wish to give a substantial amount of money to your child but do not trust his or her financial wisdom; a trust is a method of dealing with that problem.

### Definitions

A *settlor* is the person who sets up the trust and puts money, shares or property into it.

The *trust instrument* is the constitution of the trust which sets out how the trust is to be managed, how the income is to be dealt with, and what will eventually happen to the capital. The instrument is usually either a trust deed or a will which sets up the trust.

The *trustees* are the people who run the trust. They can only run it according to the trust instrument. The settlor may also be a trustee.

The *beneficiaries* are the lucky people who will or may – eventually – be given some money, either as income or as capital from the trust.

A *discretionary trust* is one where the trustees can decide who gets the money. The class of beneficiary may have been decided, eg 'all my children'. A discretionary trust may state that the trustees may pay income or capital in such proportions as they in their absolute discretion shall decide. It is usual for the settlor to guide the trustees by giving them a 'letter of wishes'. A discretionary trust is liable to IHT every ten years, and when capital leaves the trust.

A trust with an *interest in possession* is where someone has a right to enjoy the income arising in the trust. For example, if assets are left to Margaret for life, and then her children in equal shares, Margaret has an interest in possession. The children have what is called a *reversionary interest*, ie they are entitled to the assets when the interest in possession comes to an end (on Margaret's death). Another simple example of an interest in possession is where assets are left to Dennis for 20 years, and then to Carol – in which case Dennis has an interest in possession, but Carol has a reversionary interest.

The person who has an interest in possession is often called a *life tenant*.

### 12.15 The tax consequences and advantages of a trust

#### The tax consequences

*1. Inheritance tax*
The inheritance tax consequences depend on the type of trust into which assets are gifted.

A gift into a trust where an individual has an *interest in possession*, or into an *accumulation and maintenance settlement trust*, or into a trust for *disabled persons* is potentially exempt transfer. This means no IHT is payable if the settlor survives for seven years. An *accumulation and maintenance settlement trust* is a special trust for children under the age of 25, and is described more fully in Section 12.16.

A gift into any other trust would be liable for IHT. Discretionary trusts are also subject to further charges of IHT every 10 years, and again when the assets are distributed to the beneficiaries.

*2. Income tax*
Income tax on a discretionary trust, where no one has an interest in possession, is at a total rate of 35 per cent (25 per cent basic rate tax plus 10 per cent additional rate tax). Trusts with an interest in possession, however, normally pay tax at 25 per cent of their income. When trustees pay income to a beneficiary, the beneficiary receives a tax credit of either 35 or 25 per cent. If the beneficiary pays tax at a lower rate, he or she can claim back the difference from the Inland Revenue. If the beneficiary is a higher rate taxpayer, then he or she will have to pay more tax on receipt of the income from the trust. Trusts are also liable to capital gains tax for gains over £2500 in a tax year. The rate of capital gains tax is the same as for income tax and is:

| | |
|---|---|
| For discretionary and accumulation trusts: | 35% |
| For interest possession trusts: | 25% |

## Some advantage of trusts
1 It can be an advantage to transfer appreciating assets into a trust to reduce the value of your estate, giving the intended beneficiary an interest in possession and reversionary interest whereby there will be no further inheritance tax to pay on the appreciation of the assets.
2 Trusts are particularly good where you want to reduce the value of your estate without making an outright gift of the assets to someone whose financial acumen is questionable.
3 The accumulation and maintenance trust has a variety of advantages (see Section 12.16).
4 As income accumulated within a trust is charged at no more than 35 per cent, it is beneficial for an individual with capital surplus to his requirements who pays tax at the higher rate of 40 per cent to transfer assets to the trust.

## Blackstone Franks' verdict
Trusts have a role to play in a variety of circumstances. Before

setting up a trust, the capital gains tax and inheritance tax implications must be considered. Remember also that once you have decided to set it up, it is not usually possible to reverse the decision.

## 12.16 Accumulation and maintenance settlement trusts

An *accumulation and maintenance trust* (A&M) has several tax advantages, and is commonly used as a way of putting assets into trust for your children while saving tax.

Capital (ie cash, property, shares etc) is gifted to the trust. No matter how much capital is gifted, there is no inheritance tax unless the donor dies within seven years. The income made by the trust is accumulated (ie kept in the trust). Any income which is not accumulated must be used for the 'maintenance, education or benefit' of the children; school fees, holidays and clothing can be paid for by the trust. Assuming the child has no other income, up to £2785 can be paid without there being any tax charge for each child. If tax has been paid by the trust, that tax can be reclaimed as a result of paying income to the child.

The trust can come to an end between ther child's eighteenth and twenty-fifth birthdays. At that point, the property is shared out. If you do not want the capital to be placed in the hands of the child, you can arrange for the trust to give the child the right to the income instead, while the capital would be given at a later date, eg by the age of 45, or earlier at the discretion of the trustees. You can be a trustee.

If the original capital of the trust is provided by the parents, any income paid out will count as the parents' income until the child is 18 or married.

The trust is liable to income tax at basic rate (25 per cent) plus the additional rate (10 per cent), a total of 35 per cent. Any income paid out for the education or maintenance of the child is treated as the child's income but deemed to be paid after deduction of 35 per cent tax, and may give rise to a tax refund. £1000 of school fees paid by the trust is regarded as £1538 of income to the child, and if the child's total income is under £2785 (the personal allowance) a refund of £538 is due to the child.

There is no inheritance tax when the capital is paid out of the trust to the children. There is no periodic charge to inheritance tax.

### Blackstone Franks' verdict

An excellent way for a higher rate taxpayer to create tax-free income for the child. The 1986 Finance Act has allowed unlimited funds to be paid into such a trust without inheritance tax being due, and the trust could include the shares in a family company. In the right circumstances, this can be an excellent device for saving tax and making investments.

## 12.17  Wills in the UK

### Introduction
A will made in the UK by a UK domicile will cover the disposition of all UK and non-UK assets, other than immovable land and buildings.

Thus a person dying in Spain, who is domiciled in the UK, leaving only a UK will, creates a problem over his or her Spanish properties. It is better, therefore, to have two wills: one for the UK, and one for Spain.

The consequences of dying without a will can be very serious over assets in the UK. Any will made before a marriage, or remarriage, is ineffective – you have to make another one. If you die without a will, there are set rules as to where your estate goes. The advantage of having a will is that your estate will be distributed as you want it to be, the administrators of the estate will be chosen by you, there may not be any unnecessary inheritance tax liability, and the estate is likely to be distributed faster at lower costs.

Professional advice should be taken to ensure that all the estate is properly disposed of, and partial intestacy is avoided. Careful consideration should be given to what happens if the person to whom you are leaving your estate (eg your wife) dies just before, or at the same time, as you. You should also be aware that a dependant has a right to make a claim against the estate if reasonable financial provision is not made for that person. You may wish to create a trust on your death if, for example, you want the income to go to your spouse, but the capital to go to your children when your spouse dies (see trusts, Chapter 14).

### Discretionary will trusts
A will trust allows the trustees to determine how assets are distributed. Of course, a 'letter of wishes' left by the deceased would be given due consideration. During your lifetime, you can alter the 'letter of wishes' easily without having to remake your will formally. The trustees have to make the dispositions within two years of the date of death if they are to be treated for IHT purposes as if made on death.

## Dying without a will

If you die without having made a will, your assets will be distributed according to the rules of intestacy. These rules often lead to an unexpected distribution of your estate. The intestacy rules in England are:

*1. Deceased is married with no children*
The widow or widower receives:

- (a)  all personal possessions
- (b)  first £125,000
- (c)  one half of everything else in the UK.

The remaining half goes to the deceased's parents. If no parents are alive, the individual's brothers and sisters (or their issue) will share the half-share. If there are no brothers or sisters or their issue, the widow or widower will take both shares.

*2. Deceased is married with children*
The widow or widower receives:

- (a)  all personal possessions
- (b)  first £85,000
- (c)  a life interest in a trust of one-half of everything else.

The remaining half passes to the deceased's children in equal shares, who will also inherit the first half when the surviving spouse dies. The surviving spouse may redeem the life interest when all the beneficiaries are adults as the whole estate may then be distributed.

   If the deceased leaves no spouse, but children, the estate is divided among the children equally.

*3. Unmarried, no children*
The entire estate passes to the parents. If no parents are alive, the estate passes to the nearest surviving relatives in the following order:

   (a)  Brothers and sisters
if none:  (b)  children of (a)
if none:  (c)  grandparents
if none:  (d)  aunts and uncles
if none:  (e)  the Crown.

*4. Common law wives*
They have no benefit under the intestacy rules, though anyone

dependent on the deceased can make a claim for financial provision under the Inheritance (Provision for Family and Dependants) Act 1975.

### A valid will – English law

There are important requirements to meet if a will is to be valid.

1 The will must be signed in front of two witnesses, who also sign.
2 Gifts made to a witness (or spouse of a witness) are invalid, though the will is still valid.
3 A witness cannot be blind, mentally ill, or under 18.
4 Where there is doubt about the mental capacity of the testator, it is advisable that a registered medical practitioner witnesses the will.
5 Any additions or alterations should be initialled by everybody.
6 Nothing should be clipped or stapled to the will.

### UK inheritance tax considerations

There are various considerations to be taken into account in drawing up your will:

- How much to leave to your surviving spouse, as opposed to using up your tax free limit of £118,000.
- Whether property should skip a generation, and be left for your grandchildren, to avoid further IHT on transfer from your children to theirs.
- Leaving property IHT free to charities, museums etc.
- How an estate which includes agricultural property relief or business property relief should be divided up.

### 12.18  Death benefits

Death benefits under company pension schemes and retirement annuity contracts are often payable into the estate of the deceased. This swells the value of the estate, and can lead to higher IHT being paid.

To avoid this additional tax, the benefits can be written under trust, for example, to your children (unless your spouse survives you by 30 days, in which case it is paid to her). In such a case, if both you and your spouse died within 30 days of one another, the death benefits would be free of IHT.

Death in service benefits in a company scheme usually include a lump sum of four times final salary. The death in service benefit of a retirement annuity is usually the return of all premiums, plus interest.

## 12.19  Paying IHT and informing the Inland Revenue

A tax return on gifts over £10,000 individually, or where the total of gifts exceeds £40,000 in the past seven years, must be made. A tax return on assets passing on death must also be made, unless the value of the estate is less than £40,000 and the deceased was UK domiciled and had made no lifetime gifts. A person *receiving* a gift may be liable to make a tax return.

The tax return must be made to the Capital Taxes Office. In England the address is Minford House, Rockley Road, London W14 0DF. In Scotland it is 16–22 Picardy Place, Edinburgh EH1 3NB. In Northern Ireland it is Law Courts Buildings, Chichester Street, Belfast BT1 3NU.

Generally, returns must be submitted within 12 months from the end of the month the gift is made, or 12 months from the end of the month of death. Penalties for late or incorrect returns can be imposed.

On lifetime gifts, the *recipient* is liable to IHT if you die within seven years unless your will says otherwise.

On your death, the tax is usually due within six months or interest is payable. Instalments are allowed on some types of property.

The accounts have to be submitted to the Inland Revenue by your personal representatives or donees or trustees.

## 12.20  Seventeen ways to avoid UK inheritance tax

### 1  Giving it away tax free
If you give away no more than £118,000 there is no inheritance tax to pay. After seven years, you can give a further £118,000 (and so on every seven years and one day). Both husband and wife have their own £118,000 limit. In addition, each year, you (and your wife) can give away £3000. Thus over a period of seven years and one day you can give away:

|  | Husband<br>£ | Wife<br>£ | Total<br>£ |
|---|---|---|---|
| 2 × £118,000 | 236,000 | 236,000 | 472,000 |
| 8 × £3000 | 24,000 | 24,000 | 48,000 |
|  | 260,000 | 260,000 | 520,000 |

## 2 Giving away 'in consideration of marriage'
Each parent can give away an additional £5000 to a child or £2500 for a grandchild and £1000 to anyone else on the recipient's marriage. The rules are very strict and professional advice on how to do it should be taken – in advance of the marriage. See Section 12.5.

## 3 Normal income expenditure
Regular amounts can be gifted as 'normal expenditure out of income' representing perhaps as much as 10–50 per cent of annual income *free of IHT*. See Section 12.4.

## 4 Unlimited lifetime transfers to individuals or trusts
You can give *unlimited* amounts to any other individual during your lifetime or to most trusts (but not discretionary trusts). The gift could be money, or shares in a company, or any other asset. However, there may be a capital gains tax problem. Provided that the recipient is UK resident, capital gains tax can be avoided by signing a hold-over relief election as long as the assets are business assets. There may be no capital gains tax to pay if the donor is both not resident and not ordinarily resident. In the event of the donor dying within seven years, there will be IHT to pay but at reduced rates. If he dies within three years of the gift, there is no tax reduction. These trusts can be very useful for giving wealth to grandchildren under the age of 25.

## 5 Avoid 'reservation'
Gifts 'with reservation' will not be exempt from tax under 4 above. The gift must be given absolutely. A gift where the donor enjoys any interest or rights is not acceptable. Thus the gift of a house, with rights for the donor to reside, is not an absolute gift, nor is the gift of shares with the right to exceptional salary from the company. So avoid giving anything which has reservation of interest. This is a very technical area. It is possible to carve out for oneself a right to reside in the house prior to making the gift. Professional advice

should be sought before attempting such a gift and remember that under the 1989 Budget proposals capital gains tax may be due.

### 6 50 per cent discount

Even if you are going to pay the tax, if you give away *before* your death, the tax rates are halved (maximum 30 per cent instead of 60). If you die within three years of the gift, the rates applying at death are used.

### 7 Keep the back door open

You could give away any amounts into a discretionary trust, where you are *not* a beneficiary, but other relatives – including your wife – are the named beneficiaries. You could remain as the controller of the assets in trust (called the trustee). A series of trusts is recommended for technical reasons. As long as your gifts are within the limits set out in (1) above, there will be no IHT due.

Your wife can also establish a similar series of trusts.

Professional advice must be sought to see whether or not any capital gains tax is due.

### 8 Life insurance

Life insurance can be a surprisingly cheap way of covering any eventual IHT bill. For example, if your estate was worth £330,000, you and your wife were aged 50, and you leave all your assets to her on your death, the IHT payable at the second death would be £84,800. For an annual outlay of about £900 pa, a tax free benefit under trust of over £90,000 can be obtained, and indeed is projected to be worth over £220,000 on the death, at age 85, of the survivor.

Alternatively at age 65, you could invest £25,000 in a last survivor investment bond (under trust) with life cover of a sum assured at second death of just under £100,000.

These costs can be reduced considerably by purchasing term life insurance which provides cover for a fixed number of years only. You choose how long. During the time you pay regular premiums; if you die, the policy pays out a fixed amount. If you survive to the end of the term, you get nothing back and premiums cease.

### 9 Equalising estates

If the husband's estate is worth £500,000, the IHT payable is £152,800, leaving £347,200 as the net estate. If estates are equalised between husband and wife and each wills their estate to children/grandchildren/relatives, the IHT payable is reduced to approximately £105,600, saving £47,200.

## 10 Residential property

If a donor gifts a property and continues to stay in it, or even visit it for other than short periods, the gift is treated under the 'reservation' rules, unless a commercial rent is paid.

Various solutions are possible. If a leasehold can be created on a freehold property, it is likely (but not certain) that the gift of freehold will be outside the donor's estate. Once the leasehold has expired, the donor would have to vacate the property or pay a commercial rent.

If a property can be sold and the proceeds gifted, the beneficiary could purchase a new property and allow the donor to live there rent free. Capital gains tax could be avoided subsequently if the beneficiary is not ordinarily resident or is eligible for 'dependent relative relief'.

## 11 Company shares, business assets and woodlands

Private company (ie close company) shares are eligible for a special 50 per cent business relief, ie the value is reduced by 50 per cent (or 30 per cent) for IHT purposes, for a controlling interest (which is defined as a shareholding of at least 25 per cent for this purpose) or 30 per cent for a lesser interest. Another way to reduce the value is to form another company (owned by the ultimate beneficiaries) and build this new company up in preference to the existing one. Assets used in Lloyd's underwriting or in any other business you carry on are also eligible for 50 per cent reduction.

Certain other property used by a private company or a partnership is also eligible for business relief at the reduced rate of 30 per cent. Similar rules apply to agricultural property but the rate is increased to 50 per cent if there is vacant possession. Woodlands can also qualify for the 50 per cent relief with, in addition, the timber being left out of account until it is sold.

In addition, a hold-over relief election can usually be made to avoid the capital gains tax.

## 12 Single premium bonds

An offshore investment bond can be a useful way to reduce your estate, yet retain an income. The beneficiary of the bond may be a child or grandchild instead of the investor. Inheritance tax may be payable at the time of buying the bond, but inheritance tax is avoided on any growth in value of the bond.

Alternatively, a trust can be established and an interest-free loan made to the trustees who then use the loan to purchase an investment bond. 'Income' can be taken in the form of loan repayments. No IHT is payable on the loan, and the trust fund, with the exception of any outstanding loan, remains outside the settlor's estate.

### 13  Giving away shares in newly formed companies
Making gifts of assets likely to appreciate is an effective way of reducing your estate. The gift is valued at the date it is gifted – not at the subsequent value. Giving away shares in a newly formed company to trusts for your children's benefit can make sense.

### 14  Giving away when cheap
One of the few benefits of 1987's stock market crash was that it reduced values for IHT purposes. Gifts are therefore valued lower.

### 15  Generation skipping
If your own children are already wealthy, pass your estate on to your grandchildren instead. This skips a generation, and reduces the likely IHT on your children's own death.

### 16  Writing in trust
Life insurances and death benefits from pension schemes may all form part of your estate for IHT purposes. You can set up the policy to pay the benefits direct to your children, in which case they do *not* attract IHT. If you are concerned that your wife, should she survive you, should receive the benefit, we advise that you write the policy benefit in trust for your children unless your wife survives you by 30 days, in which case she receives the benefit.

### 17  Interest-free loans
An interest-free loan is *not* a gift as long as:

   (a)  the loan is documented
   (b)  the loan is repayable on demand or on very short notice.

Such loans can be used to purchase assets from the donor. Professional advice should be sought before granting such loans.

*Chapter 13*
# The UK Tax Implications of Working in Spain

## 13.1 UK income tax

If you work in Spain and live there for a period of less than one year, you will normally remain liable in full to UK tax.

If you work in Spain for a period of at lest 365 days (regardless of whether or not this covers a complete tax year), you will be exempt from UK tax on those earnings. This is regardless of your residence status in the UK. The performance of some duties in the UK will not cause this relief to be lost as long as the duties are merely incidental.

The Inland Revenue take a harsh line, however, on the meaning of 'merely incidental duties' and the more senior the employee, the harder it is to establish that UK duties are 'merely incidental'. Visiting the UK to report to your boss is usually regarded as incidental. Attending a board meeting, however, is not regarded as incidental. The Revenue will look at the *quality of the duties* undertaken in the UK rather than the time spent on them to determine whether or not they are 'merely incidental'.

This relief is not given to the self-employed – only to the employed. (But some tax planning points for the self-employed are set out on page 178.) There is a trap, though. To achieve your 365 days of continuous employment abroad, you cannot during that period:

- spend more than 62 days continuously in the UK for any reason
- spend days in the UK which in aggregate exceed one-sixth of the length of the total period under consideration.

Note in particular that just avoiding spending more than 62 days in the UK is *not* the rule. You must also avoid the 'one-sixth' rule.

A day will be considered to be a day of absence if you are outside the UK at midnight. If your flight leaves the UK at 11 pm in the evening, that is normally regarded as an entire day spent abroad, although there is no legislative basis for this and it is accordingly unwise to rely on it. If you return from abroad at 11 pm, even after a hard day's work, the legislation provides that this must neverthe-less be taken as a day in the UK.

The one-sixth limit is applied very rigidly. An unplanned or unexpected visit to the UK can spell disaster in trying to establish the 365-day minimum period. Careful planning is required, as shown in the following example:

|  | Date | Days abroad | Days in UK | Total days |
|---|---|---|---|---|
| Leaves UK for Spain | 12.8.87 | | | |
| Returns to UK for Christmas | 15.12.88 | 125 | | 125 |
| Leaves UK for Spain | 20.1.89 | | 36 | 161 |
| Returns to UK for grandfather's funeral | 7.2.89 | 18 | | 179 |
| Leaves UK for Spain | 10.2.89 | | 3 | 182 |
| Returns to UK | 10.12.89 | 304 | | 486 |

The number of days spent in the UK between two periods of absence cannot exceed one-sixth of the total number of days in the period under consideration. In the above example, the individual spends 486 days from the time he leaves to work in Spain to the end of his assignment. On returning to the UK on 7 February 1988, there is a total period of 179 days. One-sixth of 179 is 30, but he has spent more than this in the UK as he was there for 36 days. Thus, the period from 12 August 1987 to 20 January 1988 is *not* a qualifying one. The calculation now starts again on 20 January 1988. He spends 18 days abroad, then three days in the UK, and finally 304 days abroad before returning permanently. Since this is a total of 325 days and is less than the required 365, the entire period of 486 days does not count as exempt from UK tax. Instead, UK tax is payable in full even though this taxpayer has been on an overseas assignment which lasted about 16 months.

### Exception for seafarers
There is one exception to the 62-days and one-sixth rules. From 6 April 1988, in the case of British seafarers, the 62 consecutive days and the one-sixth intervening days have been increased to 90 consecutive days and one-quarter respectively.

### Tax planning
An interesting tax planning opportunity can arise on the employee's return to the UK. When the tour of duty in Spain ends, the employee could have a period of paid leave as part of that

employment, before taking up his new appointment. By leaving the overseas country before the paid leave begins, he will probably no longer be taxable in the foreign country. Any income arising in the period of leave is not taxable in the UK either if the individual does not return to the UK until after the leave period has ended. (It is possible to return before, but professional advice should be taken.)

For the expatriate working abroad, the realisation of profits on any share options while overseas should be considered. If they are unapproved (ie liable to income tax), gains arising while not UK resident are, in practice, not taxed in the UK. If approved options, the gains are UK tax free while not resident and not ordinarily UK resident in the UK.

If you are self-employed, consider forming your own limited company to employ your services and to take advantage of the 365-day exemption. Professional advice should be taken.

### 13.2  Company pension schemes

If you are still employed by a UK company, you should check how long you can continue to contribute to your UK company pension scheme.

If you are seconded from your UK company, you can normally remain in the UK scheme for at least three years. After that your employer should seek Inland Revenue approval.

If you are sent abroad to work for any other type of employer, including the non-resident subsidiary of a UK group, you should consult your employer and a professional adviser.

You will probably find it beneficial to remain in your UK scheme. If that is not possible, you should consider transferring your UK scheme entitlement to an overseas scheme.

Finally, you should check whether your employer's pension contributions, if you are subject to tax in Spain, are taxable in that country. (Previously, as a UK taxpayer, you would not be taxable on your employer's contributions.)

### 13.3  Personal pension schemes

Check with your independent financial adviser whether it is best for you to continue with your personal pension scheme and for how long and what other conditions and/or restrictions may apply.

### 13.4 Life assurance

As stated in question 20 of Inland Revenue form P85 (which is reproduced in Section 8.5), if you move abroad your entitlement to pay premiums net of tax relief may be affected. Non-UK residents must pay premiums gross (even if the policies were taken out before 14 March 1984) and you should tell your bank and life office of your departure.

Check your life assurance policies because you may not be covered for death in service while you are abroad. Consider taking out extra cover, perhaps term life assurance, to cover your foreign stay because of your changed circumstances.

### 13.5 Personal accident and sickness insurance

This would insure you against accident or sickness, the benefits being in the form of either a lump sum or an income. The payments are made following death, loss of sight or a limb, or on permanent total disability. Unfortunately, the contract is of an annual nature and subject to your state of health at the beginning of each year and can therefore be cancelled by the insurance company. Any lump sum paid is usually free of tax, but income benefits are treated similarly to those from permanent health insurance policies, ie they are tax free until they have been received for one complete tax year.

These policies are not as good as permanent health insurance (see Section 13.7) because they can be cancelled, but they should be considered.

### 13.6 Private medical plans

There are over 5 million people covered by private medical insurance. The purpose of these plans is to enable you to obtain certain medical treatment privately rather than through the National Health Service. This means that you can usually select the time you want the treatment; you can select a hospital convenient to you and even possibly choose a particular surgeon; you can obtain benefits such as a private room with television and telephone and more flexible visiting hours. Some policies provide a daily cash benefit to pay for incidental expenses while in hospital, such as telephone calls.

The main companies providing cover are BUPA, PPP, Western

Provident Association (WPA), Health First and Bristol Contributory Welfare Association (BCWA). These companies are constantly changing their premiums and policy terms. There are group plans available which can be cheaper.

BUPA is the giant of the private medical business with some 70 per cent of the market. PPP is its nearest rival, with WPA and BCWA following some way behind.

### The elderly
Remember that the policy is only an annual one – the insurers can refuse to renew your contract. BUPA, PPP and WPA will not take on new members over the age of 65. All three companies have age bands with different premiums and the cost of cover can increase dramatically with advancing years. BCWA will allow new members to join up to the age of 69. PPP has a special Retirement Health Plan for which the upper age limit for joining is 75. It only comes into effect if there is a waiting list for a bed in an NHS hospital for more than six weeks, but this seems a reasonable compromise.

### Discounts
You can often get discounts by paying by direct debit or by being a member of a group scheme or of a professional organisation. Company schemes usually offer excellent discounts.

If you and your family are not put into a private medical scheme by your employer, consider joining one yourselves. These policies, however, can be difficult to obtain and they can be expensive, particularly if you are elderly, and they will almost certainly exclude cover for pre-existing conditions. Cover may be available from a UK company and some addresses are given in Appendix 1.

You should always ensure that your policy covers evacuation in cases of serious ill health or where specialist treatment is required but unavailable locally.

### 13.7 Permanent health insurance

In a year male workers are seven times more likely to be away from work for more than six months than they are to die. The insurance which can soften the blow of long-term illness or disability is misleadingly called permanent health insurance. It offers nothing of the sort but, once you sign up, the insurance company is bound to keep you on the books, however sickly you become, and however recurrent your condition.

Permanent health insurance provides a replacement income up to pension age to substitute income lost through prolonged sickness or disability, which is often defined as 'unable to perform any part of normal duties'. Payments may start after a deferred period of a minimum of four weeks, but this is more likely to be at least 13 weeks. The premiums are reduced if the deferred period is extended. The premiums depend on occupation, the age of entry, whether you are male or female, and the deferment period, and are fixed once the contract is in force. The maximum benefit payable is normally 75 per cent of salary (less a single person's basic national insurance invalidity pension). Benefits are tax free up to the end of the first complete tax year; thereafter they are classed as unearned income. This should not be confused with sickness and accident insurance where the benefits are paid out after eight days, are tax free, only last for 104 weeks, and premiums may be increased each year although renewal can be refused if disability has occurred.

The contract cannot be cancelled by the insurance company, neither can it refuse to renew the contract if your health deteriorates. Note that different companies can have different definitions of disability – some are harsh, while others take a more lenient approach. Policies are usually written to the age of 60 or 65 and benefits will cease at that age even if the disability continues. The level of insured benefits can either remain constant or increase in line with the retail price index or by a fixed percentage.

If your employer does not include you in a scheme or pay the premiums, consider taking out cover yourself. A policy usually guarantees a continuation of your income in the unfortunate event of long-term disability and is suitable for those working abroad. Cover and benefits vary but the protection is a must for the working expatriate.

## 13.8 UK capital gains tax

This can be avoided if you are not resident and not ordinarily resident. See Chapter 9.

## 13.9 UK capital gains tax – your own home

This is a very complex subject but worthy of careful study if tax on your home is to be avoided. The matter is covered in detail in Section 10.8.

## 13.10 National insurance contributions

### Social security and pension schemes

The system of UK social security known as national insurance is administered by the Department of Social Security (DSS) through a network of local offices around the country and specialist offices.

Wherever you, or your employer, have any overseas involvement your national insurance contribution position can become very complicated. All such matters are the responsibility of the DSS Overseas Branch whose address is given in Appendix 1.

The rules provide that an individual working within a Community country is to be subject to contribution legislation of only one state, which will normally be that in which he is employed or self-employed, and not the state in which he may be resident. However, when the employment in the state is less than 12 months and the individual is not replacing a person whose period of employment has come to an end, the individual may remain liable to contributions in the state of residence.

*Self-employed outside Great Britain.* An individual in self-employment outside Great Britain can make class 2 contributions if, immediately before he last left Great Britain, he had been an employee or was self-employed and either

- he has been resident in Great Britain for a continuous period of three or more years at some time prior to the contribution period; or
- he has paid contributions above a prescribed limit in each of any three earlier tax years.

### Summary

If you are employed by a UK company abroad, you will normally have to continue paying national insurance contributions for 12 months even though you may not be paying UK tax.

If you work in an EC country, such as Spain, or one with a reciprocal agreement with the UK, you may join the social security scheme of that country. However, if you have to continue to pay UK contributions, you should get a certificate of continuing liability by writing to the Overseas Branch of the DSS; the address is given in Appendix 1. This certificate (retain a photocopy) should be given to your overseas employers, otherwise they may deduct local social security from your salary.

If you are in any doubt, consult a professional adviser.

## 13.11 Benefits and medical care in the European Community and abroad

Booklet SA29 (October 1987), *Your Social Security Health Care and Pension Rights in the European Community*, available from the DSS, tells you about insurance and contributions as well as what benefits you may get and how and where to claim them. Booklet NI38, *Social Security Abroad*, is a guide to national insurance contributions and social security benefits outside the European Community and countries with which the UK has reciprocal agreements (mentioned in (2) of Section 13.10). Booklets are available from the DSS for each of the countries with which the UK has a reciprocal agreements.

Generally speaking, entitlement to UK benefits is affected by absence abroad. Some benefits can be paid abroad only in certain circumstances and there are restrictions on entitlement to benefits as a result of events, such as accidents at work, that happen while working outside the UK.

Medical treatment under the National Health Service is available only in the UK and no reimbursement of foreign medical costs can be made.

European Community social security regulations apply to periods spent by UK citizens in other EC member states. The regulations apply only to employees and recipients of UK benefits who were formerly employed, together with their dependants and survivors. Self-employed people are generally excluded from the scope of the regulations. However, there are also reciprocal arrangements between the UK and other EC countries (except Greece), by which self-employed individuals may be covered.

## 13.12 Taking your car abroad

You can buy a car in the UK, and take it overseas, and avoid paying the UK VAT on the car. You should check whether or not you have to pay VAT or its equivalent in your new country. Car security can be a problem in many countries, so consider having a good alarm system fitted. Sun roofs and air-conditioning can be very useful in hot countries. People moving to Spain often choose diesel-powered vehicles as diesel is half the price of petrol and easily available there.

### New purchase
To make a tax-free export, you have to comply with the VAT export scheme. You have to buy the car from the manufacturer or sole UK

selling agent. (The car can be a British or a foreign one.) He will give you a form VAT 411 to complete and you must:

1 undertake to go abroad for at least 12 months (though you can bring the car back for temporary visits);
2 take the car abroad within six months of buying it. You may use it in the UK up to then;
3 keep the car for your use abroad for 12 months before selling it or allowing someone else to use it.

Remember that the car can be seized by Customs and Excise *and never returned* if you break any of these rules. Even if the car is stolen, and is in the UK when it should be abroad, Customs can seize and keep it. After 12 months abroad, you can re-import the car to the UK and not pay VAT. You should insure it for its full value (ie including VAT) until the 12 months abroad period has ended.

**Existing car**
You cannot obtain a VAT refund, except as described above for new cars.

If you take your existing car abroad, leaflet V526 is very useful. It is available from your local Vehicle Licensing Office. Complete section 2 on the back of the Vehicle Registration Document, entering the proposed date of export, and send it to your local Vehicle Licensing Office well in advance of your departure. They will issue a Certificate of Export (V561). The rules for Northern Ireland or the Isle of Man are slightly different.

# Chapter 14

# Trusts in Tax Planning

## 14.1 Introduction

Trusts or settlements (the two words are interchangeable for all practical purposes) are one of the earliest and still probably the most efficient tax planning tool. Successive governments have introduced legislation to discourage the use of trusts in tax planning, starting with the Statute of Uses 1535, which was designed to inhibit the use of trusts to avoid feudal dues, and continuing to this day. In spite of this, the trust has continued to flourish. The reason is undoubtedly that a trust can provide great flexibility. Since a trust is a separate legal entity, it can be used in estate planning to hold assets in suspense; in capital gains tax planning to avoid time apportionment or artificial identification rules; in income tax planning to reduce the effective rate of tax; and, by changing its residence, to defer income tax and capital gains tax, often for long periods or indefinitely.

Trusts are not just for the super-rich. They can be used for relatively modest sums: around £20,000–25,000 may be quite adequate for an accumulation and maintenance trust to provide the deposit on a flat for a child when he or she reaches the age of, say, 25. Similarly, assets which have a low value now but a potentially high value in the future (eg shares in your business) can be sheltered from capital gains tax by the use of trusts.

Offshore trusts are often used to avoid tax as they involve many valuable tax privileges, and a close study can reveal many ways of using them to advantage.

A trust is where one person (the settlor) transfers an asset to another (the trustee) to be held on behalf of a third person (the beneficiary). It is not necessary to enter into any formalities. A trust need not be in writing although it is usual, and highly desirable, to have a written trust deed.

The trust deed sets out the powers of the trustees and governs the circumstances in which they can pay income or capital to beneficiaries and frequently specifies what proportion of the trust property can be paid to an individual beneficiary. In the event of a dispute, the settlor's intentions at the time the trust was set up can often be determined by the provisions that he put into the trust deed.

A trust deed can be a fairly daunting legal document as it can easily run to 20 or 30 pages. It needs to be drawn up with extreme care as serious adverse tax consequences can arise if certain rules are infringed and, if the deed is badly drafted, circumstances can arise in which it is not clear for whose benefit the property is held. If your solicitor is not experienced in drafting trusts, it is safest to use a specialist trust solicitor.

It is usual to have at least two trustees, although this is not a legal requirement unless the trust owns land. But it is sensible as if you have a sole trustee problems will obviously arise should he die.

Before we discuss how such trusts operate, here is a reminder of the meaning of some of the technical terms which will be used in this chapter.

**Beneficiaries** The lucky people who may or will, eventually, be given income or capital from the trust. There is nothing to stop the settlor (or the settlor's spouse) being one of the beneficiaries.

**Discretionary trust** The trustees can decide who will receive income or capital. They are usually restricted to a class of persons (eg, 'relatives of X' or 'all X's children'). They may also pay regard to a 'letter of wishes' from the settlor.

**Letter of wishes** A letter written by the settlor to the trustees setting out his wishes as to how the trust is managed. Such wishes can be ignored by the trustees who are not legally bound to follow the wishes. Verbal wishes may also be made.

**Offshore trust** A trust controlled from a tax haven, such as the Isle of Man, Channel Islands, Panama, Andorra etc. This means the majority of trustees are resident in a tax haven.

**Reversionary interest** The entitlement to the trust assets after the person(s) who have the interest in possession.

**Settlor** The person who set up the trust.

**Trust** A separate legal entity governed by a document (the trust deed) which was drawn up by the settlor, and managed by the trustees.

**Trust with interest in possession** A trust where the income has to be paid to one or more individual(s), and the trustees have no discretion as to how the income is divided. The right to the interest in possession is sometimes known as the *life interest*, and the person with the life interest sometimes referred to as the *life tenant*.

**Trustees** The people who manage the trust. They can only run it according to the trust deed.

## 14.2 The discretionary offshore trust

Most offshore trusts are discretionary ones. Usually all (or a majority) of the trustees are foreign trustees, not resident and not ordinarily resident in the UK. In addition, none of the administration takes place in the UK or Spain. This does not prohibit the trust from using UK resident advisers, however, such as chartered accountants, investment managers, stockbrokers etc. The final decisions must be taken by the offshore trustees, and the administration must not be undertaken in the UK.

In the event of political unrest, it should be possible for the trust to be transportable to another tax haven.

Usually, there are no government reporting requirements for trusts located in tax havens. Thus there is usually no register of trusts, and no tax to pay in the tax haven provided none of the beneficiaries is resident in the tax haven, and no income arises in the haven itself. If structured carefully, there will be no taxes to pay within the trust, thus allowing income to be re-invested tax free.

If the settlor dies, the assets in the trust are usually free of all capital taxes. The beneficiaries' enjoyment of the trust income and capital remains at the discretion of the trustees, who will usually have regard to the wishes of the deceased settlor. Thus there are no complicated foreign probate regulations to deal with. Income paid by the trust to a Spanish resident would be liable to Spanish tax.

If a beneficiary goes to live in a highly taxed area, he can request that the trustees reduce the level of payments to him.

## 14.3 An offshore company

An offshore company is usually one which is incorporated in a tax haven (eg Jersey). However, many people mistakenly believe that such a company can be free of tax in the UK or Spain, for example. Even though a company is incorporated in, say, Jersey, it can still be tax resident in the UK or Spain. It is a matter of where, in reality, the company is *managed and controlled* which usually determines its residence. If you live in Spain, and own a Jersey company which is managed and controlled by you, that company can be liable to Spanish taxes on its worldwide income.

Usually, an offshore company is owned, managed and controlled by the offshore trust. This breaks the legal ownership chain between the settlor or beneficiaries and the company. The trustees must genuinely manage and control the company. The offshore company does not have to be incorporated in the same country as that in which the trustees are resident. Indeed, often the two are different. The trustees will ensure that the shares are issued, hold regular meetings, update the company's statutory and accounting records and manage the company's bank account properly.

The offshore company can be a trading or an investment operation. A company is often used to own assets, rather than the trust, as it is a separate legal entity, and usually a simpler medium in which title to assets can be bought and sold.

## 14.4 UK inheritance tax (IHT)

If the settlor of an offshore discretionary trust is UK domiciled, gifts into the trust over the £118,000 limit are liable to UK IHT. If the gift is subject to business property relief, £236,000-worth of shares can be transferred into the trust. If your spouse is also eligible for business property relief, a total of £472,000 can be transferred into the offshore discretionary trust every seven years free of IHT.

If the settlor is not domiciled in the UK, there are no limits. Thus someone who might lose their foreign domicile status would be well advised to pass assets into an offshore discretionary trust sooner rather than later.

As explained in Chapter 12, unlimited gifts can be made into trusts which have an interest in possession. As long as the settlor survives for seven years, no IHT is payable. Advice should be taken on the capital gains tax position.

Where the settlor himself has an interest in possession (called a 'settlor trust'), there is no IHT due. On the settlor's death, IHT would then be payable, as IHT is due when the settlor's life interest terminates.

Where an offshore trust is created by a UK domiciled settlor (regardless of residence), the settlor and the advisers involved in setting up the trust have an obligation to inform the UK Capital Taxes Office. This is so even if only £10 is placed in trust.

## 14.5 UK capital gains tax

### Taxation of trustees
As long as the trustees are all (or a majority) non-UK resident, no UK capital gains tax is payable, even if the assets are located in the

UK. Thus even the sale of a property in the UK held by the trust as an investment is free of UK capital gains tax.

**Taxation of beneficiaries**
Gains made by the offshore trust (called 'trust gains') are not immediately chargeable to UK capital gains tax. If part of those trust gains are then paid to a UK resident, the beneficiary is taxed on the trust gains.

There are three ways the tax can be avoided, even though payments are made to UK residents:

- pay income only to UK beneficiaries, not capital. Reinvest the capital with the trust, or pay it to non-resident beneficiaries;
- if a beneficiary becomes non-UK resident for a complete UK tax year, trust gains can then be paid to him free of UK capital gains tax; and
- if a non-UK resident beneficiary receives trust gains in one tax year, and then in a subsequent tax year he pays part or all of the trust gains to a resident beneficiary, no UK gains tax is due.

**Taxation of settlor**
If the settlor is not resident and not ordinarily resident, or has the protection of the double tax treaty, no capital gains tax is payable on the gift into the trust.

The hold-over election is not available if the trust is offshore.

### 14.6 UK income tax

**Taxation of trustees**
If *none* of the trustees are UK resident, there is no UK income tax except on income arising in the UK.

If *some* of the trustees are UK resident, the position is not clear. It is therefore better if all trustees are non-UK resident.

**Taxation of beneficiaries**
If the settlor is UK resident and UK domiciled, he will be taxed on all the trust income, whether or not it is paid to him. This can be avoided if the settlor is rigorously excluded from the settlement so that it is impossible for him to benefit. In that case, income can be rolled up into the trust free of UK income tax. Thus the offshore trust is even a tax-free device for UK residents.

If a UK resident receives any benefit from the trust, he will be subject to UK income tax.

191

## 14.7 Spanish tax position

Spanish income tax is on worldwide income. Income which arises in offshore companies outside Spain, owned by offshore trusts, not under the control of a Spanish resident, is not liable to Spanish tax. Thus the underlying assets are also free from Spanish inheritance tax and exchange control regulations. Professional advice on the Spanish tax system should be taken before any offshore trusts are set up.

## 14.8 Exporting a UK company

New rules about exporting a resident UK company were introduced in 1988. The former requirement of having to obtain Treasury consent to change a company's residence from the UK to overseas was abolished. If a company wishes to migrate from the United Kingdom, it will now be required not only to settle its tax liabilities (as the Treasury in practice required as a condition for giving consent under the old rules) but also to pay tax on accrued but unrealised capital gains on assets held at the date of transfer of residence.

*Chapter 15*
# Personal Financial Planning and Investment

## 15.1 Introduction

This chapter is intended as general guidance on investment matters for individuals who own property in Spain. Such individuals normally fall into the following three categories:

- UK residents who are also UK domiciles, ie those individuals owning holiday homes in Spain.
- Non-UK residents, UK domiciled, ie those who are British by birth and retain their domicile of origin but who have relocated to Spain on a permanent/semi-permanent basis.
- Non-UK residents, non-UK domiciled, ie those who live permanently outside the United Kingdom and who have a foreign domicile of origin.

Becoming non-resident can have a major implication for your investment strategy and personal financial planning. This chapter highlights some of the important differences which need to be taken into account.

## 15.2 Tax and exchange control

The taxation tail should not wag the investment dog, but the investment which is safe and is tax protected is to be preferred.

UK residents can invest anywhere in the world since 1979 when exchange control was abolished. However, you have to be careful that you do not export your capital from the UK into a new country which imposes exchange control; you may never get your capital out again. Spain imposes exchange control.

## 15.3 Investment objectives

These are usually:

A need for income
A desire to increase capital values.

These requirements are provided by establishing either an income-producing portfolio or a portfolio designed to obtain capital growth. More often a portfolio of investments is established to provide a combination of each of these two requirements.

For individuals taking up residence in Spain the most important consideration is that the capital base from which income is to be provided cannot be recreated. The capital available for investment is often the result of a life's labour or a benefit from UK pension schemes and is, therefore, required to be invested in an extremely secure fashion to provide capital protection and realistic levels of income throughout life. A combination portfolio, therefore, providing reasonable levels of income, while ensuring an acceptable rate of growth, is normally the order of the day for retiring expatriates.

It is important to consider as part of the investment objective the tax implications in relation to the manner in which investments are structured.

One of the major problems in holding a portfolio of investments which are registered in the beneficial ownership of married partners is that upon the death of either partner, probate will be required before the title of the investments can be transferred to the survivor. For this reason investments are often held in a nominee name.

In selecting the investments to provide a balance between income and capital appreciation, the following are the most commonly considered investments:

- High interest offshore bank and building society deposits;
- UK gilts, Eurobonds and other triple A rated fixed interest securities with short maturity dates;
- High yielding gilt and fixed interest offshore funds;
- International equities;
- Income and growth offshore funds.

The normal strategy for investment portfolios of up to £250,000 is almost certainly to use a well-diversified range of pooled funds to ensure a cost-effective geographical, sector and currency spread.

For investment portfolios over £250,000 it can prove more cost effective to include certain direct investments including equities and fixed interest securities where the management of these investments is dealt with by an independent financial adviser.

Most UK nationals retiring to Spain hold their investments

# What's Sound Advice and Absolutely FREE?

## The Target International Tape

As an expatriate with money to invest, are you sure what types of plan are right for you? Your individual investment needs are like yourself, unique.

No doubt you've been bombarded by packaged schemes and promises to make your money grow.

To help you pick your way through the confusion we're offering some sound advice that's absolutely *free*.

As an established leader in the UK Financial Services industry, we're well qualified to do this. Our Tape, an audio cassette, will tell you everything you need to know about today's investment market, Target Group and Target International's investment services. It's yours, when you fill in the coupon and send it to us.

We cannot tell you what you need to know in the space of an advertisement and your completed coupon here will hardly give us a comprehensive picture of your needs.

So with the Target International Tape we'll send a questionnaire. Return it to us, and we'll put together a proposal designed to meet your personal investment needs, and based upon the expert advice of the best independent specialists in Britain. Again that's *free* and no obligation is implied.

Further counselling from independent professional advisers can also be arranged.

If you hear something telling you to complete the coupon now, could it be the voice of reason?

### TARGET INTERNATIONAL (EUROPE) LIMITED

mainly in pounds sterling, with a limited amount of investments held in pesetas, normally on deposit. However, currency fluctuations become a major consideration when you decide to retire abroad. Should your investments be in Japan, Germany, USA, UK? If currencies are to be part of your investment mix, in what proportions should they be held? Just because you are used to the UK does not mean that your investments will do best in the UK or invested in sterling. As an international resident the world markets are now at your fingertips, and you should be benefiting from that wider choice.

## 15.4 Investment media for non-residents

### Cash and bank deposits
UK bank accounts should be avoided because:

- of potential reintroduction of exchange control if political changes occur in the future;
- by concession, UK bank and building society interest is not taxable on non-residents, but you have to prove your non-residence to the Inland Revenue;
- for the non-domiciled, UK deposits may be liable to UK inheritance tax.

Overseas bank accounts which pay interest can be denominated in most major currencies (deutschmark, yen, dollar, pound) and may be an ideal home for monies before investing permanently.

Even for UK residents, it may be advantageous to retain monies overseas should exchange controls be reintroduced (and repatriation of overseas monies not enforced).

*Credit cards and bank statements*
Non-residents usually receive an international Visa credit card with their offshore bank account. The credit card can be used anywhere in the world, and monthly settlement made direct from the offshore bank account.

Credit card statements and bank statements are often required by a tax authority where there are disputes over residence. A credit card statement is often good evidence of when visits were made to the UK, for example.

### Building societies
Building societies have similar disadvantages to UK bank accounts

for non-residents. However, many building societies now have offices in Jersey, the Isle of Man and Gibraltar providing high interest paid gross.

## National Savings

National Savings are excellent for UK residents, especially those liable to UK tax; but they are a poor investment for non-residents who can earn higher yields overseas. They also lock you into UK rates of return.

## Gilts

There are special gilts for non-residents which are tax free. You have to prove your new residence to the Inland Revenue. Gilts are safe but suffer from some of the same disadvantages as UK bank accounts.

## Foreign government securities (ie non-UK) and Eurobonds

These securities offer a fixed rate of return and have differing maturity rates. Any fixed rate investment can fall in price as well as rise. Eurobonds are issued not only by other governments but by large corporations. Some – but not all – pay interest without deduction of tax. There are funds which specialise in the purchase of Eurobonds since most investors lack the ability to manage such funds actively.

## Stock Exchange

The investor can be faced with a bewildering range of choices, since he can invest in any one of over 20 major stock exchanges throughout the world. This allows the investor to spread his risk in two ways:

*Geographic spread*
The main markets are:

> USA
> Japan (and Far East)
> UK
> Continental Europe.

By having a geographic spread, the investor can have two new features in his portfolio: currency and a different economic base. Investing in Japan, for example, means you will benefit from the strength of the yen; thus even if the underlying Japanese investments did not increase in value in yen terms, a gain can be recorded if the yen continues its phenomenal growth. Often a country which has a strong currency also has a growing stock market.

*Sector spread*

Having chosen your geographic spread, you have to select the investment sector. Sectors are usually classified as: banks, breweries, building and timber, chemicals, stores, electricals, engineering, foods, hotels/caterers, industrials, insurance, leisure, motors, paper, printing and advertising, property, tobaccos, oil and gas, plantations and mines. In addition, there are usually smaller company sectors.

## The personal portfolio bond fund

This arrangement represents a major advance in the field of investment management. The personal portfolio bond is technically a life assurance contract. In practice, it is a highly effective framework within which your own personal investments may be held. Your portfolio is established consisting entirely of your own private and personally selected holdings. This may be built up from a wide range of investments drawn from any of the world's fixed interest or equity markets. The investment fund may also include interest-bearing bank deposits or building society accounts. Indeed this facility may even receive stock transfers from your existing holdings.

This arrangement is only available from a few selected independent financial advisers or directly from certain major offshore international life assurance companies.

The administration, dealing and valuation procedures are handled by a major institutional investment house offshore which means that the taxation of your investment profits is reduced to the absolute minimum. You are able to retain the investment advisory skills of your appointed independent financial adviser.

As the portfolio of investments held within the bond is technically structured as a life assurance policy, it may be established from the outset on the joint lives of, say, married partners. In this case there is no change of beneficial ownership on the date the first marriage partner dies and this can have considerable taxation advantages in Spain. Indeed it is possible to write such an arrangement to include the children of a retired couple and the bond will then continue to hold certain tax advantages even after the death of the survivor of the married couple.

The personal portfolio bond provides for a simple means of producing income on a regular basis by withdrawing income and capital growth from within the bond and remitting this by, say, direct transfer to an offshore bank account which may then be used to transfer income to Spain as required.

The personal portfolio bond may be subject to a separate simple declaration of trust which will indicate how the benefits of the portfolio are to be distributed on the death of the individuals who own the bond. No probate will be required in either Spain or the UK in these circumstances, thereby avoiding the normal extensive delays.

The personal portfolio bond may also be of benefit for expatriates who have established an investment structure while living overseas but who then decide to return to the UK. Within the UK, provided the bond meets certain criteria, a 5 per cent withdrawal facility which is free of both personal income and capital gains tax may also apply for up to 20 years.

Perhaps one of the most important features is that the investments within your portfolio and any uninvested cash are held by a major institution or insurance company providing total security for these hard-earned assets.

The tax position of these bonds in Spain is not absolutely clear and opinions vary. It is believed that no Spanish tax is due unless a withdrawal is made, in which case only a proportion of the withdrawal is liable to tax. If the bond's investments have grown by 10 per cent, for example, only 10 per cent of the withdrawal would be liable to tax. The bond, like all personally owned investments, should be disclosed on the Spanish wealth tax return.

**Authorised UK unit trusts**
Since income arising on authorised UK unit trusts is taxable on the non-resident, whereas capital gains are not, the best unit trusts for non-residents are often those directed towards capital growth.

A capital growth unit trust will aim for a low level of income. There are over 1000 authorised UK unit trusts to choose from. Offshore funds should generally be preferred by the non-resident to ensure that there is no UK tax exposure.

**Offshore funds**
Offshore funds, unlike authorised UK unit trusts, are not subject to the authority of the Securities and Investment Board. You should therefore select a fund managed by a well-known, large institution. As mentioned above, the tax position for non-residents investing in offshore funds is better than for investing in UK authorised unit trusts. One result of the increased freedom given to offshore trusts

# INVESTMENT SERVICES
## W·O·R·L·D·W·I·D·E

MIM Britannia International Limited, based in Jersey since 1971 is part of Britannia Arrow Holdings PLC which is a United Kingdom public company.

The MIM Britannia group manages investments valued in excess of £20 billion world wide and has offices in London, Jersey, Paris, Isle of Man, Gibraltar, Monaco, New York, Denver, Boston, Atlanta, Tokyo and Hong Kong.

Investment clients include pension funds, unit trusts, mutual funds, institutional and private clients.

MIM Britannia International is one of the largest investment management companies in Jersey and offers a wide range of offshore investment funds and services specifically designed for the needs of international investors.

MIM Britannia's world-wide resources and expertise are available to you through our sales office in Gibraltar, so whatever your investment objective, high income, income and growth or capital growth MIM Britannia International can help you.

Just complete and return the coupon below or telephone direct. All enquiries will be treated in the strictest confidence and there is no obligation.

## (GIBRALTAR)

2nd Floor, Neptune House, Marina Bay, Gibraltar.

Telephone: (9567) 79756/79781 Telecopier: (9567) 78654

Name (in capitals)

Address

LS   89

Tel. No.

*All enquiries will be treated in the strictest confidence*

*A member of the Britannia Arrow Group*
*Investment Services Worldwide*

is that they have considerably wider investment powers than are permissible for UK authorised unit trusts.

The taxation suffered by the offshore fund itself (as opposed to tax paid by the non-resident investor in the fund) is a complex matter. It depends on where the fund is resident, where it invests, and the availability of double taxation agreements. Generally, funds are resident in tax havens, and tax haven countries rarely have double tax treaties with other countries. Thus the fund receives income after tax is paid in the country in which the investment is made, but capital gains are tax free. An offshore fund concentrating on capital growth, and resident in a tax haven (eg the Channel Islands, the Isle of Man), is likely to make and pay its gains with only a minimal amount of taxes deducted.

### Endowment policies and investment bonds
Generally, these are not appropriate vehicles for the non-resident investor (other than specific offshore versions which can be especially favourable).

## 15.5 Legal title to investments

There are two types of ownership to any assets. First, the registered title, which means the name (or names) in which the investment is registered. This could be an individual, a company, a bank, a nominee company, etc. Second, the beneficial title, which means the name of the real owner entitled to the assets. The legal and beneficial owner can be the same: for example, assets which you own, and which are in your name, are both legally and beneficially owned by you. On the other hand, it can often be advantageous to have a different legal title (eg a nominee company) from that of the beneficial owner (you). The advantages of using a nominee company are efficiency in dealing on your behalf by your investment adviser and confidentiality.

## 15.6 Choosing an investment manager

### Do you need a manager?
Many individuals owning a property abroad, whether UK resident or non-resident, run their own investment portfolios successfully and derive great enjoyment from it. They may be in the financial investment business or it may be a hobby in retirement. Others

have neither the time nor the experience to manage their investments, and their money ends up languishing in high street banks and building societies.

Most individuals with capital, and owning property abroad, need a financial adviser and, sooner or later, an investment manager. What is the difference between a financial adviser and an investment manager? Many financial advisers adopt a 'freeze frame' approach in that they look at the current position, make what may be sound recommendations (commonly allied to their selling the investments concerned), go away, then perhaps return at a later stage to repeat the process with the funds then to hand. An investment manager, on the other hand, has a continuing responsibility to manage the funds. He will usually manage numerous funds for many clients, thus spreading his costs among his clients. He is always thinking of his clients and adapting to the changing markets.

## How do you choose?

How do you find such an adviser–manager? Whom should you choose? There is no single or simple answer. It is possible, if somewhat unlikely, that the 'one-man band' operating out of a hotel room somewhere in Benidorm is the most superb and talented investment manager around. On the other hand, the bigger, better known institutions are often impersonal and provide a second-class service to their individual clients who are secondary to their corporate accounts.

Choosing an investment manager is more of an art than a science, and ultimately the decision is likely to be made on a subjective rather than an objective basis. Nevertheless there are certain guidelines which can be followed.

### Costs

Management fees are commonly in the range 0.5–1.5 per cent of the value of the portfolio per annum, with minimum charges of between £250 and £500 per annum. Professional management is rarely offered on sums of below £50,000.

### Quality

The quality of service should not vary with the size of portfolio, but it is a fact of life that certain managers will devote little time to a portfolio of less than £100,000. There is a tendency for portfolios of under £100,000 to be invested in unit trusts or offshore funds. On cost considerations alone this may be to your advantage when compared to the expense of direct investment.

Investment managers come in all shapes and sizes but those most frequently used by non-UK residents tend to be drawn from one or other of the following categories:

- investment advisers based offshore where they are part of a larger financial institution;
- independent investment advisers (FIMBRA members);
- stockbrokers (mainly UK or US based);
- banks (clearers, merchant, Swiss or American).

By using a UK-based adviser you will enjoy the full protection of the UK investor protection legislation, the Financial Services Act. If you appoint offshore advisers, especially individuals who have themselves 'retired' to Spain and continue to provide investment services, you will have no statutory protection if they go broke on you!

You might usefully write to one or two advisers in each category for details of the services they provide. This information should include details of charges (how much and how calculated), the track record of funds under management, and whether or not this is mainly individual or personal cash or institutional, eg pension funds. Basic company data should also be provided with details of any subsidiaries, in-house funds, and links with other institutions. From this initial information you should be able to pick the most likely adviser and then arrange a suitable meeting. At the initial meeting you should seek to find out precisely how and by whom your portfolio will be managed, what degree of independence of action the individual managers enjoy or whether they follow a committee dictate.

Independent investment advice is always to be preferred, as you are more likely to receive objective recommendations in attempting to meet your objectives. Many institutional advisers and tied agents offer in-house products which are often inferior.

Assuming everything else is satisfactory, of greatest importance to the investor will be his personal relationship with the prospective manager.

A final word of caution: in evaluating a manager's performance, do not take the first three months as conclusive. Any fund manager deserves at least a year to show his true investment ability.

*Chapter 16*
# School Fees Planning

## 16.1 Introduction

About half a million children attend private schools in the UK, with fees per term ranging from £380 to £2500. Private schooling costs have always been high, but a recent survey showed that families whose children were going to private school were not necessarily high earners. About half the parents had an income of less than £25,000 per annum, with some as low as £10,000. A number of children are from families living outside the UK.

Whichever method is used to fund school fees, the following matters should be taken into account:

1  The possibility of the child not going to private school.
2  The possibility of the child changing to a different school midstream.
3  Death or incapacity of the child.
4  Possible increase in costs because of inflation.
5  The possibility of the abolition of private education.
6  Deterioration of the parents' financial circumstances.
7  Death of the parents.
8  Break-up of the marriage.

There are three major sources for funding school fees; we analyse each of these below.

## 16.2 From capital

You pay a lump sum to an insurance company or a broker or a school, and the money is invested in a variety of ways. Some schemes have some tax advantages (in particular the school fees composition schemes and educational trusts).

The three main types of capital scheme are as follows:

### School fees composition schemes
You pay a lump sum to a school representing school fees paid in

advance. The school then invests the money, usually in an annuity which starts paying out when the child goes to school. The amounts you have to invest will vary from school to school depending on the fee levels and the discount you might be given for paying in advance.

These schemes are essentially deferred annuity contracts. Because the school enjoys charitable status, its income is free of tax. The school pays the lump sum over to an insurance company in return for an annuity which, in the hands of the school, is tax free. The scheme is thus particularly attractive to a higher rate taxpayer since he would not be liable to either income tax or capital gains tax arising from the investment of the lump sum by the school. If he purchased the annuity instead, there would be income tax to pay.

The size of the discount which the school is able to offer will depend largely on the length of the period before the fees become due and the level of interest rates at the time the lump sum is paid.

Advice should be taken on the inheritance tax position of the parent or any other relative who makes the lump sum payment.

One of the main advantages of the school fees composition schemes is that they are reasonably simple to formulate and convenient to operate. However, they can be very inflexible. For example, a repayment might be made if the child does not attend the school, but usually on very unattractive terms. Schemes vary as to what happens if the child leaves the school or dies before his education has been completed. A parent should also discuss the position if the advantages relating to educational charities are abolished in the future.

## Educational trusts

Educational trusts are designed to overcome some of the disadvantages of the school fees composition schemes, since they are independent versions of the school fees composition schemes or created by the schools themselves. You can usually switch funds from the benefit of one child to the benefit of another (which may not be the case with school fees composition schemes), and you do not have to nonimate the school to which the fees are to be paid until shortly before the child starts school. If the child dies before the end of the plan, the amount paid into the plan, less any school fees payments already made from the plan, is usually repaid under the trust deed.

The tax advantages of the deferred annuity contract being paid to an educational trust are the same as for the school fees composition scheme, and this scheme is therefore attractive from this point of view.

### Fixed interest schemes

The lump sum is applied to purchase suitable fixed interest investments such as British government stocks, local authority bonds and National Savings certificates. It may also be possible to make use of any existing investments owned by the payer. The purpose of the scheme is to ensure that, as far as possible, the investments mature shortly before the necessary funds are required to pay the school fees.

These schemes are generally more flexible in that the investments are not restricted for educational purposes – the money can be used for anything else if circumstances change. However, it can take some time to work out a worthwhile scheme and the income would be taxable.


### 16.3  From income

There are a number of different ways in which these schemes can be set up, but most involve saving regularly by taking out investment-type life insurance policies, ending year by year as the fees become due. Thus the payments are spread over a longer period than the period of education. The amount of monthly savings is obviously *less* if you start these policies later rather than earlier. The scheme should also include some insurance in case the income provider dies early, becomes disabled or is made redundant.

There are three main methods of school fees planning out of income, described below.

### Life assurance schemes

These are essentially endowment policies. An ordinary term life assurance pays your estate a lump sum on death, but pays nothing if you survive the agreed period. An endowment policy not only pays a lump sum on death, but pays you a tax-free lump sum at the end of the term. In other words, you are bound to get your money back (either dead or alive!). The lump sum can be guaranteed, so you know exactly how much you, or your estate, will receive. An endowment is a way of saving, but you must save for at least seven and a half years (and possibly longer) to avoid extra tax charges. You can pay monthly, and the lump sums are used to fund the school fees. Life assurance schemes can be very effective.

### Unit trust regular savings plan

This can be either a straightforward unit-linked savings plan or can represent direct investment into unit trusts on a regular (usually monthly) basis. In the latter case, no life cover is provided and consideration should be given to this separately. A unit trust savings plan provides greater flexibility than a unit-linked savings plan since it may be terminated at any time without penalty. Capital gains tax on realisations and income tax on income would be payable.

### Deferred annuities through an educational trust

This is similar to a lump sum investment in an educational trust, except that, rather than paying a lump sum to an educational trust, premiums are paid monthly. Each premium purchases a guaranteed level of fees provided by way of a deferred annuity arranged through an educational trust.

### 16.4 Other sources

Apart from meeting the costs of school fees from your own capital or income, the following ways may be open to parents:

- A deed of covenant from relatives, especially grandparents.
- Borrowing – you may be able to arrange a loan based on the security of your home or other investments or based on investment-type life insurance policies.
- If the parent is a partner in a trading partnership, it may be possible to arrange for a lump sum to be withdrawn from the partnership but replenished by a bank loan. Tax relief might be obtained on such a loan.
- A loan could be made against your pension funds.
- Setting up an accumulation and maintenance trust fund with grandparents' money (not the parents') has tax advantages.
- As a last resort, capital might be released by moving to a cheaper house.

### 16.5 Local authority grants for university or polytechnic students

The rules for obtaining grants from a UK local authority for your child's education in the UK, while you reside outside the UK, are complex. You should always consult your own local authority to ensure that your child is eligible for a grant.

To be eligible for a grant, there are two key points which the expatriate parents must establish:

1 that your residence abroad is intended to be a temporary one and that you intend to return to the UK;

2 that your child is intent on pursuing a full-time education course in the UK.

As you can see, intention to return is important.

It can be difficult to determine to which local authority you can apply for the grant. You apply to the local authority where the child is 'ordinarily' resident on 30 June prior to the commencement of any course in the autumn term (or 31 October or 28 February if the course starts in spring or summer).

If there is no 'ordinary' residence in the UK, the location of the local authority is determined as the area where the student has been 'ordinarily' resident at any time in the two years before 30 June (or 31 October or 28 February if spring or summer terms).

If there has been 'ordinary' residence, you apply to the local authority in the area where the student had any physical residence before 30 June (or 31 October or 28 February). This would usually be the area in which the student's school is located.

If there was no physical residence, you apply to the local authority in the area where the university or polytechnic is located.

There are two kinds of course, designated and discretionary:

### Designated courses

These include most university, polytechnic and teacher training courses. They are 'designated' by the Secretary of State for Education and Science. Grants are *mandatory awards*, ie the local authority *must* pay the grant if your child is accepted on the course. (In fact, 90 per cent of the grant is paid by central government.) Mandatory awards include fees for tuition, registration, admission, matriculation, examination and graduation. College fees are covered for the universities of Cambridge, Oxford, Durham, Kent, York and Lancaster.

### Discretionary courses

These might include one-year secretarial courses, foundation art courses, nursery nursing courses and Ordinary National Diploma courses. The local authority does *not* have to pay a grant, and usually only pays for those students who have done well in the exams.

You should apply for grants as early as possible; do not wait for your child to be accepted. When you apply, include with your application form a letter setting out your personal circumstances in detail, including:

- your reason for living outside the UK;
- how long you intend to be abroad;

- how long you have been abroad;
- the courses your child is applying for;
- child's age and school performance;
- where school holidays have been spent;
- where college holidays might be spent;
- whether or not you have a UK home;
- why you think your child is eligible for a grant;
- remember that your intention is to return to the UK soon so emphasise the temporary nature of your period overseas.

Usually, there are three forms which need to be completed:

*Application form* Includes exam results, career goals of child, and headteacher's assessment.
*Income form* Includes your full income and addresses for third-party confirmation (eg accountant, employer). If divorced or separated, the parent with whom the child lives should completed the form.
*College acceptance form* Completed by the college.

The local authority mandatory or discretionary award only covers the fees mentioned above. It does not include residence costs (eg board and lodging), deposit moneys, materials or equipment. Maintenance grants are available for these costs, but they are means-tested, and most expatriates earn too much.

*Chapter 17*
# Your Spanish Home: Should a Company Own it?

## 17.1 Introduction

Whether or not you put the ownership of your property into a company, it is important to instruct a good lawyer in Spain to deal with the legal title problems, as mentioned in detail earlier in this book.

It is a very popular move these days to put the Spanish property into a company, and this chapter explores the advantages and disadvantages of so doing. If you do proceed to purchase through a company, professional advice must be sought.

## 17.2 Advantages

### Selling advantages
More and more foreigners in Spain seem to insist on purchasing a company owning a property, not a property direct. It may therefore be easier to sell your property via a company, *though this could change.* If the Spanish decided to hit foreign company ownership hard, the last thing anyone would want to purchase are shares in an offshore property owning company.

### Exchange control
If by buying and selling shares in an offshore company you avoid buying (or your purchaser avoids buying) domestic pesetas, then there is an exchange control advantage. Note that this is not always the case. For example, two non-resident Spanish individuals can always buy/sell a Spanish property without having to deal in domestic pesetas.

### Property taxes
By selling a company instead of a property, the purchaser has no property transfer taxes to pay. This is because the ownership of the

property itself is not changing. It is only the ownership of the company which alters.

## Capital gains tax

A Spanish resident is liable for income tax on his worldwide gains. If he sells shares in an offshore company, tax on the gain is due. (The roll-over reliefs for individuals owning in their own name would not be given if the property was owned by an offshore company.) However, if the shares were owned by an offshore company trust, there is no tax on the capital gain in Spain on the sale of the shares.

If the property – rather than the shares – were sold for offshore monies (not domestic pesetas) by a Spanish non-resident, while the capital gain may be technically taxable in Spain, the *Hacienda* does not usually raise a tax assessment. The tax, in these circumstances, would be almost impossible to collect if the vendor has no other assets in Spain. This is not the case if domestic pesetas are paid for the villa; the *Hacienda* would then be able to collect the tax on the gain successfully. The tax rate is 35 per cent for non-residents.

## Distribution on death

If a trust owns the shares in the company, it is usually far easier for the trustees to distribute the shares on the death of the settlor. The legal costs of winding up an estate in Spain are complicated. If instead the shares were owned by a trust, the estate could be wound up more easily.

## Confidentiality

If a company owns a property, there is much greater confidentiality. If you own the property personally, anybody can go to the Land Registry and discover your name.

## Spanish inheritance tax

If you die and leave a legacy of the shares in the offshore company to your wife, for example, and she is resident in Spain, Spanish inheritance tax will be payable. This is exactly the same position as if the property itself were left to your wife. If you leave the shares to someone who is not resident in Spain, there will be no Spanish inheritance tax. If the shares in the offshore company are owned by a trust, and your wife is a beneficiary of the trust, on your death there is no transfer of assets. In other words, there is no inheritance tax. It is therefore advisable to have an offshore trust own the offshore company shares.

## 17.3 Disadvantages

### Plus valía
Where property is owned by a non-Spanish company or foreign trust, there is a deemed disposal of the land on every tenth anniversary and *plus valía* is then payable. No *plus valía* is payable if instead you own the property in your own name until it is sold.

### Company liabilities
If you purchase a company which already owns the property you wish to live in, you could find other unexpected liabilities in the company, and you would be responsible for sorting them out. Take careful professional advice to ensure that the company has never traded and that you are indemnified in full by the vendor. If you use a company, do not put any other assets or business into it.

### Offshore company tax
The offshore company is liable to tax at 35 per cent on what is in effect the market rental it could receive for the property. In practice, this tax is usually not pursued, but this could change in the future.

### Inherent tax
The company may be liable to pay tax on the gain made on the eventual sale of the property. If you buy shares in a company from another person, that company may be liable to an eventual capital gains tax liability based on the original cost of the property, which is not the same as your original cost of the shares. You have thus taken over an inherent tax charge.

### Costs
You will have to pay anything from £500 per annum to keep the company going, and more to form it.

### France?
Spain may go the same way as France which introduced a 3 per cent annual tax on all properties owned by foreigners. This effectively killed off foreign company ownership, and left company owners high and dry.

### Return to the UK?
If you ever return to the UK (or you remain a UK resident), the structure of a company owning your Spanish residence can be a UK tax disaster. The Inland Revenue can tax you personally on:

- rental value of property; plus
- 20 per cent of value of furnishings owned by the company; plus
- a notional interest charge if property cost exceeds £75,000; plus
- any expenses paid by the company.

It is possible to avoid these charges if a trust owns the company, but advice must be sought in this tricky area. The eventual sale of the property may give rise to a UK tax liability. Another way to avoid the benefits in kind charge is to make the company solely a nominee company for the individuals, who are the beneficial owners. A trust document (or nominee agreement) would be needed.

## UK inheritance tax
If you did not own the company, but gave the company sufficient funds to purchase the property, you may be liable to the UK inheritance tax.

## Gibraltar company?
The Spanish authorities are very sensitive about Gibraltar. Having a Gibraltarean company can be seen as provocative. If you were to use a company, you should consider using one incorporated elsewhere.

## Transfer existing property?
If you transfer a Spanish property which you already own into an offshore company, the following conditions apply:

1 You will be liable to income tax on the capital gain made on selling to the company (even though you own the company). Market values will be used.
2 Before transferring the property to your offshore company, you must prove to the Spanish authorities that the company has funds to purchase the villa. Having received approval, you then sell the property to the company and receive pesetas. You will not be able to re-export those pesetas back into a hard currency.
3 If you try to avoid Spanish taxes by undervaluing the property, you can be subject to substantial fines. Indeed, the Spanish Supreme Court can purchase the property from the company at the lower price if they consider the underdeclaration to have been substantial.

## UK residents
If you reside in the UK, and you want to transfer a Spanish property

into a company you control, then:

- you are liable to the same benefit in kind charges mentioned above;
- UK capital gains tax based on the market value of the property will be payable;
- if you transfer at above market value, UK income tax is payable on the excess; and
- other directors/employees staying in the property can be taxed heavily on the benefit in kind.

### The offshore company

It is important that the property-owning company does not trade, and exists *only* to own the property. Otherwise, it will be impossible to sell the shares in the company as no one would buy them if there had been a trading history.

### Spanish income tax

Where an individual applies for a longer form of Spanish residential permit, among the evidence required is ownership of property. The permit may be denied if the property is owned by an offshore company, thus jeopardising Spanish tax residence confirmation for double tax treaty purposes.

### Deductions

There are certain deductions against income given to individual house owners resident in Spain which are not available to corporate owners.

# Appendices

# Useful Names and Addresses

**Bank of England**
Threadneedle Street
London EC2R 8AH

**Blackstone Franks** – UK
Barbican House
26–34 Old Street
London EC1V 9HL
Tel: 01-250 3300
Fax: 01-250 1402

**Blackstone Franks** – Spain
Daioz y Velarde No 6
Edificio Beneco 2ªy3ª
Apartado de Correos 159
29640 Fuengirola
Malaga
Tel:   010-34-52-479400
       010-34-52-462021
       010-34-52-461085
Fax:   010-34-52-476246

**British Embassy** – Spain
Fernando El Santo 16
Madrid 4
Tel: 010-34-1-419-02-12

CONSULATE GENERALS – SPAIN
**British Consulate General** – Algeciras
Avenida de las Fuerzas
Armadas 11
Algeciras
Tel: 010-34-56-66-16-00

**British Consulate General** – Alicante
Plaza Calvo Sotelo 172–1
Apartado 564
Alicante
Tel: 010-34-65-21-60-22

**British Consulate General** – Barcelona
Edifico Torre de Barcelona
Avenida Diagonal 477–13
Apartado 12111
Barcelona 36
Tel: 010-34-3-322-21-51

**British Consulate General** – Bilbao
Alameda de Urquijo 2–8
Bilbao 8
Tel: 010-34-4-415-76-00

**British Consulate General** – Ibiza
Avenida Isidoro Macabith 45–1
Apartado 307
Ibiza
Tel: 010-34-71-30-18-18

**British Consulate General** – Las Palmas
Edificio Hocasa 6
Calle Alfredo L Jones 33
Puerto de la Luz
Apartado 2020
Las Palmas
Las Canarias
Tel: 010-34-28-26-25-08

**British Consulate General** – Madrid
Fernando el Santo 16
Madrid 4
Tel: 010-34-1-419-02-12

**British Consulate General** – Malaga
Edificio Duquesa
Duquesa de Parcent 4–1
Malaga
Tel: 010-34-52-21-75-71

**British Consulate General** – Mallorca
Plaza Mayor 3D
Palma de Mallorca 12
Tel: 010-34-71-21-24-45

**British Consulate General** – Santander
Paseo de Pereda 27
Santander
Tel: 010-34-42-22-00-00

**British Consulate General** – Seville
Plaza Nueva 8
Seville
Tel: 010-34-54-22-88-75

**British Consulate General** – Tarragona
Santian 4
Tarragona
Tel: 010-34-77-20-12-46

**British Consulate General** – Tenerife
Edificio Marichal 5
Suarez Guerra 40
Santa Cruz de Tenerife
Tel: 010-34-22-24-20-00

**British Consulate General** – Vigo
Plaza Compostela 23–6
Apartado 49
Vigo
Tel: 010-34-86-21-14-50

**BCWA**
Bristol House
40–56 Victoria Street
Bristol BS1 6AB
Tel: 0272 293742

**BUPA International**
Equity & Law House
102 Queens Road
Brighton BN1 3XT

## Department of Social Security
Overseas Branch
Benton Park Road
Newcastle upon Tyne
NE98 1YX

## Information Division
Leaflets Unit
Block 4 Government Building
Honeypot Lane
Stanmore
Middlesex HA7 1AZ
Tel: 01-952 2366

(DHSS – Spain)
## Instituto Nacional de la Seguridad Social Subdireccion General de Relaciones Internacionales
Padre Damian 4
Madrid 16

## Health First (Sun Alliance)
Richmond Hill
Bournemouth BH2 6LQ
Tel: 0202 292464

## Inland Revenue
(a) for payments of pensions or dividends overseas:
Inspector of Foreign Dividends
Inland Revenue
Lynwood Road
Thames Ditton
Surrey KT7 0PD
Tel: 01-398 4242

(b) for booklets:
Public Enquiry Room
Inland Revenue
West Wing
Somerset House
London WC2R 1LB

**Institute of Foreign Property Owners**
38 Hillfield Road
London NW6 1PZ
Tel: 01-431 2499
Fax: 01-431 2467

**National Association of British Schools in Spain**
Arga 9 (El Viso)
Madrid 2

**Ombudsman** – Spain
Calle Fortuny 22
28010 Madrid

**Private Patients Plan**
Eynsham House
Tunbridge Wells
Kent TN1 2PL

**Spanish Chamber of Commerce**
5 Cavendish Square
London W1M 0DP
Tel: 01-637 9061

**Spanish Consulate General** – London
20 Draycott Place
London SW3 2RZ
Tel: 01-581 5921

**Spanish Consulate General** – Manchester
1 Brooks House
70 Spring Gardens
Manchester 2
Tel: 061-236 1233

**Spanish Consulate General** – Scotland
63 North Castle
Edinburgh EH3
Tel: 031-220 1843

**Spanish Embassy**
24 Belgrave Square
London SW1X 8QA
Tel: 01-235 5555

**Spanish Embassy**
Commercial Office
22 Manchester Square
London W1M 5AP
Tel:01-486 0101

**Spanish National Tourist Office**
57–58 St James's Street
London SW1A 1LD
Tel: 01-499 0901

**Western Provident Association**
Rivergate House
70 Redcliffe Street
Bristol BS1 6LS
Tel: 0272 225677

**Solicitors Specialising in Spanish Law**

**Diaz-Bastien & Truan**
111 Park Street
London W1Y 3FB
Tel: 01-491 3308
Fax: 01-629 2902

**John Howell & Company**
427–431 London Road
Sheffield S2 4HJ
Tel: 0742 501000
Fax: 0742-500656

**Michael Soul & Associates**
20 Essex Street
London WC2R 3AL
Tel: 01-242 0848
Fax: 01-240 0139

**Fernando Scornik Gerstein**
32 St James's Street
London SW1A 1HD
Tel: 01-930 3593
Fax: 01-930 3385

# Retirement Relief

Retirement relief is a major relief from UK capital gains tax whereby gains of up to £125,000 are free of UK tax. Fifty per cent of the gain between £125,000 and £500,000 is also tax free. There are many conditions and traps which have to be watched.

1 You must be aged 60 or over when the disposal is made. You can obtain the relief if you have been forced to retire prematurely because ill health made you unable to continue.
2 Despite the name 'retirement relief' you do not actually have to retire. You do have to dispose of:

   (a) all or part of a business. The business must have been owned for at least one year, and to obtain full relief the period is ten years; or
   (b) within 12 months of cessation of a business, assets in use in the business at the time of cessation; or
   (c) shares or securities in a 'family' trading company in which you were a full-time working director; or
   (d) an interest of a partner in the partnership assets.

3 Note that for 2(a) above (the disposal of all or part of a business) the mere disposal of a business asset will *not* qualify.

If you have owned the business for less than ten years, partial relief is given.

If the gain exceeds £125,000, after deducting indexation relief, the first £125,000 is exempt. Fifty per cent of the gain between £125,000 and £500,000 is also free of tax.

The relief is given either for:

(a) unincorporated businesses, ie sole traders or partners; or
(b) shares in a 'family' company

**Unincorporated businesses**
The business must be a trade or profession; it cannot be property letting (unless it is furnished holiday lettings meeting the conditions described in Appendix 3).

The assets must have been used in the trade and cannot include shares or securities (but see the section on a family trading company below).

If, instead of disposing of the trade, assets are sold and the business is closed, retirement relief may still be claimable. There must usually be no more than a year between closure and disposal.

Each partner is entitled to £125,000 relief, and the 50 per cent relief, even if the partners are husband and wife, though each must be over 60 and have been in the business for over ten years if full relief is to be obtained.

Assets used by a partnership, but owned by one or more of the partners, will be eligible for relief if:

- the asset is a chargeable business asset;
- the asset is disposed of as part of a withdrawal from participation in the partnership;
- the partner disposes of his interest in the partnership;
- the partner is over 60;
- the sale of the asset *does not* precede his disposal of the partnership interest (as the asset must be in use for the purpose of the partnership business immediately before disposal).

If the asset was not used for the partnership business throughout its ownership by the taxpayer, the Inland Revenue can still allow relief on a 'just and reasonable' basis.

If an asset has been rented to the partnership the Inland Revenue can deny retirement relief. If a less than market rent has been charged, part relief might be granted. Merely agreeing a higher share of profit instead of rent will not ensure that relief is granted if it is in consideration of making a property available.

Even if the taxpayer has not owned the business that he disposes of for the full ten years, he may have owned an earlier business which can be used to extend the qualifying period.

In practice, the date of disposal of assets for retirement relief purposes is taken to be the date of *completion* rather than the exchange date, where the vendor continues to run the business up to completion.

**Shares in a 'family' trading company**
To obtain retirement relief on the sale of shares in a company, the company must be:

- a trading company (or a holding company which owns a trading company);

- a 'family' company as defined;
- employing the taxpayer as a 'full-time working director' as defined.

Each of the above three conditions must be met at the date of disposal of the shares and for one year before to obtain any relief. To obtain maximum relief, the three conditions must have been met throughout the ten-year period prior to disposal; otherwise partial relief may be due. There are special rules where a company had ceased trading.

A trading company excludes property investment or any other investment activity (eg shares). The company must therefore carry on a business which is mainly a trade or trades. A holding company whose subsidiaries are all trading companies is acceptable. A subsidiary is one where more than 50 per cent of the shares are owned.

A 'family' company is one where either:

(a) 25 per cent of the votes are owned by the taxpayer; or
(b) at least 5 per cent of the votes are owned by the taxpayer *and* over 50 per cent of the votes owned by the taxpayer and his 'family'.

'Family' means spouse, parent, ancestor, child, descendant, brother or sister, and the taxpayer's spouse's parent, ancestor, child, descendant, brother or sister. A spouse does not have to be living with the taxpayer, but an ex-spouse does not count.

Votes controlled by family trusts may be included if:

(i) the trust income is for the benefit of the taxpayer or his family; *and*
(ii) no one can benefit from the capital (or income) other than the family.

A 'full-time working director' is not defined, but is generally taken to be a director working at least 25 hours a week on the company's business (or the group, if a group of qualifying companies). Partial relief may be given if the taxpayer has reduced his or her work load to at least ten hours a week as a director working on technical or management matters.

There is no requirement to own the shares for any minimum period. Thus a taxpayer who meets the above conditions, but who has purchased extra shares shortly before a disposal, can still qualify for retirement relief for all of the shares.

If some of the assets owned by the company are non-trading ones (eg investment properties), even though the company is primarily a trading company, partial relief may be due. The part of the gain eligible for relief is calculated as:

$$\frac{\text{value of chargeable business (trading) assets}}{\text{value of all chargeable assets}} \times \text{gains}$$

It can help if the company sells all chargeable non-trading assets (eg shares) for cash before the taxpayer sells his or her shares, so that the restriction on the relief is avoided.

Relief is also due if:

(a) the company ceased to be a trading company within one year of disposal. The Inland Revenue can extend the one-year rule; *and*

(b) the taxpayer was age 60 by the date of cessation, and all other conditions were met for the ten years (or at least one year for partial relief) up to cessation date.

An asset owned by a shareholder, but used by a family owned company, can also qualify for retirement relief if:

- it is a chargeable business asset; *and*
- the disposal is part of a withdrawal by the taxpayer from participation in the company's business; *and*
- a disposal of shares is also made, though not necessarily at the same time as the asset is sold; *and*
- the shares also qualify for retirement relief; *and*
- immediately before the share disposal, the asset was in use for the purpose of the business. This means the taxpayer cannot dispose of the asset *before* the disposal of the shares.

### Husband and wife

Husband and wife are each eligible for £125,000 retirement relief. In some circumstances, one spouse can acquire assets from the other, and obtain full relief even though the ten-year requirement is not met. These circumstances are (assuming the husband owned the business or shares first, though it could equally be the wife):

1 The husband transfers his whole interest (of business or shares) to his wife.

2 The transfer is by gift or as a result of death. (If by gift, there is a complex restriction of the relief.)

3 In the tax year of transfer, husband and wife must be living together.

4 When the wife disposes of the business or shares, she should have met the relevant conditions for one year.
5 The wife must claim in writing within two years of the disposal that her husband's period of ownership be aggregated with her own.

Husband and wife tax planning can be used to great effect. If, for example, the husband qualifies for full relief as a full-time working director, but the wife's shares do not (as she does not work in the company), she should transfer her shares to him prior to disposal. If they both qualify, but the husband's gain exceeds £125,000 while the wife's is less, a transfer should be made from husband to wife.

**Trust**
Trusts too can qualify for retirement relief if:

(a) there is a life tenant whose retirement relief can be used;
(b) there is a 'qualifying beneficiary' who has an 'interest in possession';
(c) the trustees dispose of assets used in the business carried on by the qualifying beneficiary.

There are other conditions required and professional advice should be sought. The terms used above are explained in Section 12.14.

**Ill health**
If a taxpayer retires early on medical advice, retirement relief can be obtained before the age of 60. Signed medical certificates will be required and the Inland Revenue will take advice from the Regional Medical Service of the DSS and may even require the Regional Medical Officer to examine the taxpayer. A claim for early retirement relief must be made in writing within two years of the end of the tax year in which the disposal is made.

All the other rules must be met. The retirement must precede the disposal, and the incapacity must be likely to be permanent. Mental incapacity also qualifies.

# Roll-over Relief: Business Assets

Roll-over relief is given under Sections 115 to 121 of the Capital Gains Taxes Act 1979. It enables an individual, or a limited company, in certain circumstances to avoid paying capital gains tax on the disposal of certain business capital assets by reinvesting in new assets. A number of conditions have to be met before the relief can be given.

## The new asset(s)

Both the asset sold and the reinvestment into the new business asset must be one or more assets in the following list:

> Land or buildings (but not if let or held as an investment)
> *Fixed* plant or machinery
> Ships
> Aircraft
> Hovercraft
> Goodwill

## Value reinvested

To obtain the relief, the investment into the new asset (or assets as it can be more than one) must be at least to the same value as the sale proceeds of the old (not just the gain). Thus if you sold for £600,000, the amount that has to be reinvested to obtain full relief is £600,000. Partial relief can be given if not all the sale proceeds are reinvested.

*Part-proceeds reinvested*
If the total cost of an asset was £200,000, and the sale proceeds £600,000, no relief would be due if the total amount reinvested was £200,000 or less. The Inland Revenue argue that the sum reinvested is merely a reinvestment of the cost, and not the gain. If instead £400,000 were reinvested, the Inland Revenue would accept that half the gain had been reinvested, and roll-over relief would be due

233

for that half. Thus only half the capital gains tax would be payable. In order to avoid paying any capital gains tax, the entire £600,000 must be reinvested.

*Time limits*
The reinvestment can occur either at any time in the three years *after* the sale of the old asset, or one year *before*. The three-year period can be extended at the discretion of the Inland Revenue, but this should not be relied upon. The date of sale would normally be taken to be the date of exchange. The claim for roll-over relief must be made within six years of the end of the tax year (or in the case of a limited company, the end of the accounting period) in which the sale was made.

**At date of sale**
It is important to note that the old asset must be used for the purpose of the trade at the *date of sale*.

You do not have to roll over into new assets of the same type as the old asset. Thus a gain on the sale of property can be rolled over into an aircraft. Nor does the new asset have to be used for the purpose of the same trade as the old.

Fixed plant or machinery would include any items which would count as landlord's fixtures under landlord and tenant law, thus lifts or central heating would be so included. Massive machinery or plant which could only be moved with enormous difficulty would also count. You *cannot* roll over into plant or machinery which does not meet these definitions, such as computers, furniture, paintings etc.

**Shares and securities and property investment**
You can never roll over into shares or securities, nor directly into property which is let as an investment. Indeed, it is a vital rule that the new asset must be used initially for the purpose of a trade. However, if you are selling shares, see Section 9.8.

**Using the asset**
It is an important rule that the old asset is used for the purposes of the trade and, where it is land and buildings, must be occupied by the taxpayer. Thus the asset cannot be let, nor can it include property development. The old asset must be used in a trade undertaken by the taxpayer at the date it is sold. The old asset must have been used exclusively for *that* trade even if not conducted by the taxpayer all the time the asset was used by the taxpayer (as long as it was conducted by the taxpayer at the time it was sold). Otherwise, the relief may be restricted.

**Staff flat**

In certain cases, the law regards the taxpayer as being the true occupier of a dwelling owned by him and inhabited by an employee or partner of his. This is called 'representative occupation'. For this to be so, it must be either:

(a) *essential* for the employee or partner to inhabit the house to carry out his duties; or
(b) an expressed term of the employment contract or partnership agreement that he does so, and that must enable him to perform his duties better to a material degree.

**Tied premises**

There are special rules in the event that you are a landlord of 'tied premises'.

**Asset owned by individual, used by company**

You can also claim roll-over relief for an asset owned by you but used in a limited company's trade as long as:

1 The company is your 'family' company. This means that as long as you own 25 per cent or more of the voting rights of the company (or if you own less, you and your family own over 50 per cent and you own at least 5 per cent).
2 The new asset is acquired by you, not by the company.
3 The new asset must be used by the *same* family company.

In other words, the new asset cannot be bought by the company; it must be bought by you. The trade cannot be undertaken by you, but the asset must be used by the company. The asset cannot be used by another company, it must be used by the same family company. It is irrelevant whether or not the company paid a rent for the use of the old asset.

**Using the new asset**

Whether a company or an individual buys the new asset, it must be used by the qualifying trade immediately it is acquired. This is a very big trap. If you wait just one week, all the roll-over relief can, in theory, be lost.

**Owning the new asset**

There are four main alternatives which, if mishandled, can lead to a loss of relief:

(a) old asset owned by individual, used in limited company trade

235

(b) old asset owned by individual, used in individual's trade
(c) old asset owned by individual, used in partnership's trade
(d) old asset owned by company, used in company's trade.

In the case of (b) the new asset *must* be owned and used by the individual in his trade.

In the case of (c) the new asset can be used either in the partnership's trade or in a new trade carried on by the individual. It can probably also be used in a new trade carried on by another partnership but the individual's share of the sale proceeds would not be fully reinvested in that individual's share of the asset in the new partnership.

In the case of (d), the new asset *must* be owned by the individual, but used in the *same* company's trade.

### Continuing to use the asset

The acquisition of the new asset must be for the purpose of use in the trade, and not wholly or partly for the purpose of realising a gain on its sale. Subject to this, however, there is nothing that requires you to continue using the new asset for the purpose of the trade throughout your period of ownership, nor is there any provision whereby the rolled-over gain becomes taxable if the asset ceases to be so used (unless the new asset is a depreciating asset as described later). Thus you could purchase a new asset, use it in the trade for, say, one year, and then merely let the asset to a third party.

### Land and buildings

Where you buy land, and then build on it, strictly speaking a roll-over relief claim cannot be made on the cost of the building. However, there are two extra-statutory concessions (D24 and D22) which have the effect of allowing roll-over relief if all the following conditions are met:

1 You propose to incur capital expenditure for the purpose of enhancing its value when you purchase the asset.
2 The work begins on the new asset as soon as possible after acquisition and is completed within a reasonable time.
3 On completion of the work the asset is taken into use for the purpose of the trade and for no other purpose (ie it must not be let or used for a non-trade purpose at that stage); and
4 The asset is at no time prior to it being taken into use used for any non-trading purpose.

These concessions also allow roll-over into the costs of improving a building (as distinct from building a new building) and into building or improving a building or land which you already own.

### 'Depreciating' assets

There are special provisions which apply to 'depreciating' assets. A depreciating asset is either one which has an expected life of 50 years or less (eg a lease of less than 50 years), or will become one within ten years. In practice, leases with 60 years or less to run, fixed machinery or plant, ships, aircraft and hovercraft are depreciating assets. You can thus obtain not only roll-over relief, but capital allowances in addition.

If you roll over into depreciating assets, the roll-over relief is not so good. You will become liable to capital gains tax on the postponed gain on the old asset at the *earliest* of the following events:

1 ten years from the date of acquisition of the new asset
2 the disposal date
3 if you cease to use the new asset for the purpose of your trade.

You should avoid purchasing any depreciating assets, and only roll over into freehold property or leases in excess of 60 years. There is one exception to this rule: if you have merely *sold* a depreciating asset, and purchased a non-depreciating asset for roll-over, the disadvantages do *not* apply.

If you do roll over into a depreciating asset, you can claim to roll over instead into a second new asset if the new asset itself qualifies and is not a depreciating asset and the new asset is bought before the tax charge on the postponed gain has crystallised. This means that you must buy the new second asset not less than ten years after buying the first, and before it has been disposed of.

### Furnished holiday lets

We said above that you cannot roll over into any property which is held as an investment and is let. There is one exception to this: the acquisition of property in the UK for letting as furnished holiday accommodation on a commercial basis is an eligible asset for roll-over relief. In order to qualify as furnished holiday accommodation the following conditions must be met:

1 The lettings must be commercial with a view to making a profit.
2 The lettings must be furnished.
3 The property must be available to the general public for periods totalling at least 140 days in the tax year and must be let for at least 70 days; or

4 The property must not normally be let to the same person for more than 31 days.

5 If the investor owns more than one property, and each property has not been let for 70 days, an averaging may be made.

6 The property must be in the UK; overseas properties are excluded.

### Second-hand assets

The new asset does not have to be new – it can be second-hand.

### Tax planning ideas

Roll-over relief can thus be made into:

- leasing trade of fixed machinery or plant, or ships or aircraft or hovercraft
- woodlands managed on a commercial basis
- furnished holiday lettings.

If the old asset was acquired before 6 April 1965, special rules apply.

### Partnerships

Assets owned by an individual, but used in a partnership trade are eligible for roll-over relief.

### Interaction with retirement relief

The interaction of roll-over relief with retirement relief (see Chapter 9) is complex and professional advice should be sought.

### Husband and wife

A husband cannot roll over into an asset acquired by his wife. However, there is nothing to stop the husband transferring part of the old asset to his wife before disposing. Indeed, if the new asset was to be acquired by the husband and was too low a price to qualify for relief, it would be beneficial to transfer part of the old asset to his wife. In this way, he may find that the sale proceeds of his smaller share are fully reinvested in the new asset, and hence he will qualify for roll-over relief. In addition, it may be worthwhile making the wife a partner in the business before selling so that she too can obtain roll-over relief.

## Partial claims

If an old asset was partly used for a trade, and partly let, partial roll-over relief would be due. Similarly, a purchase of a new asset partly let and partly used in a trade may still give you a partial claim to roll-over relief.

## Payment and interest

As you have up to three years to purchase the new assets, the Inland Revenue might still raise a capital gains tax assessment since you cannot prove you have reinvested the sale proceeds. In practice, your Inspector of Taxes will normally ask the Collector of Taxes not to enforce collection of the tax assessment. This preserves the Inland Revenue's right to charge you interest in the event that you do not reinvest.

# Glossary of Spanish Terms

| | |
|---|---|
| *abogado* | lawyer (2.4) |
| *actas* | minutes (6.9) |
| *administracíon* | administration (3.3) |
| *al portador* | to bearer (2.6) |
| *alcalde* | mayor (1.4) |
| *arbitrio sobre incremento del valor de los terrenos* | tax on increased land value (2.6) |
| *assesor fiscal* | tax expert (3.10) |
| *asociacíon de empresas en participacíon* | joint venture (6.5) |
| *Audiencia Provincial* | provincial court (1.14) |
| *Ayuntamiento* | town hall (2.4) |
| | |
| *Bolétin de Instalaciones Eléctricas* | certificate of electrical installation (2.10) |
| *Bolétin Oficial del Estado* | official estate journal (2.16) |
| | |
| *cambio de residencia* | residence application (2.13) |
| *Cedula de Habitabilidad* | habitation certificate (2.10) |
| *Certificado de Fin de Obra* | completion certificate (2.10) |
| *chateo* | lunchtime break (1.12) |
| *churros* | twisted fritters (1.12) |
| *Congreso de Diputados* | Congress of Deputies (1.4) |
| *contrato* | contract (2.4) |
| *contribucion territorial rústica* | country rates (2.9) |
| *Cuenta de Enlace* | company's annual return (5.10) |
| *contribuciones urbana* | town rates (2.9) |
| | |
| *declaración ordinaria* | standard tax return (3.3) |
| *declaración simplificado* | simple tax return (3.3) |
| *Defensor del Pueblo* | ombudsman (2.1) |
| *delegación* | delegation (3.3) |
| *demanda* | civil action (1.14) |
| *denuncia* | formal complaint (1.14) |
| *derechos y tasas sobre la propiedad inmueble* | local service charge (2.9) |

| | |
|---|---|
| *diario* | journal (6.9) |
| *Dirección General de Transacciones Exteriores* | exchange control authority (5.1) |
| | |
| *El Tribunal Constitucional* | constitutional court (1.4) |
| *empresa individual* | sole trader (6.5) |
| *escritura de compraventa* | property deed (2.3 et seq) |
| *escritura de poder de compraventa* | power of attorney (2.3) |
| | |
| *finca* | old farmhouse (2.1) |
| | |
| *gazpacho* | type of cold soup (1.12) |
| *gestor* | lawyer (2.8) |
| | |
| *Hacienda* | tax office (3.1) |
| *hecho imponible* | taxable event (3.11) |
| *herederos forzosos* | obligatory heirs (1.15) |
| *hipoteca* | mortgage (2.7) |
| *hoja de reclamación* | complaint sheet (1.16) |
| *horchata de chufas* | cold almond drink (1.12) |
| | |
| *impuesto sobre el valor añadido* | value added tax (3.1) |
| *impuesto sobre la renta de las personas fisicas* | personal income tax (3.1) |
| *impuesto sobre sociedades* | corporate income tax (3.1) |
| *impuesto sobre sucesiones y donaciones* | inheritance and gift tax (3.1) |
| *impuesto sobre transmisiones* | transfer tax (2.6) |
| *Instituto de Censores Jurados de Cuentas* | Institute of Accountants (6.9) |
| *Instituto de Proprietarios Extranjeros* | Institute of Foreign Property Owners (2.1) |
| *Instituto Nacional de la Segurigad Social* | Social Security office (7.1) |
| *inventarios y balances* | balance sheet (6.9) |
| | |
| *juzgado de la paz* | justice of the peace (1.14) |
| | |
| *Ley de Arrendamientos Urbanos* | Law of Urban Lettings (2.16) |
| *Ley orgánica sobre Derechos y Libertades de los Extranjeros en España* | law of foreigners (4.5) |
| *licencia de apertura* | operating licence (6.4) |
| | |
| *Mapa de campings españoles* | Spanish camping map (1.12) |

| | |
|---|---|
| *Ministerio de Económia y Hacienda* | Ministry of Economy and Taxation (3.1) |
| *notario* | notary (2.4) |
| *páguese al portador por este cheque* | pay bearer by this cheque (5.5) |
| *paradores* | state-run hotels (1.7) |
| *pelota* | ball game (1.12) |
| *permanencia* | residence permit (4.1) |
| *plaza mayor* | main square (1.12) |
| *plus valía* | land value tax (2.6) |
| *poliza* | police (4.3) |
| *practicante* | medical assistant (7.6) |
| *presidente* | prime minister (1.4), or chairman (2.17) |
| *privato* | private contract (2.4) |
| *quiniela* | tote (1.12) |
| *roscón* | Epiphany cake (1.11) |
| *segurigad social* | social security (7.1) |
| *sociedad anonima* | public company (6.5) |
| *sociedad colectiva* | partnership (6.5) |
| *sociedad comanditaria* | limited partnership (6.5) |
| *sociedad de responsabilidad limitada* | private limited company (6.5) |
| *sucursal* | branch office (6.8) |
| *tabacaleria* | tobacconist shop (3.3) |
| *tasas* | local service charge (2.9) |
| *tenientes de alcalde* | deputy mayors (1.4) |
| *tertulia* | evening break (1.12) |
| *testamento abierto* | open will (1.15) |
| *testamento cerrado* | closed will (1.15) |
| *usofructarios* | life tenants (2.3) |
| *valor catastral* | rateable value (3.4) |
| *vivienda secundaria* | application for second residence (2.13) |
| *y Cia* | and company (5.5) |
| *zarzuela* | musical play (1.12) |

**Index of Advertisers**

Arts International Removers *40*
Cater Allen Bank (Jersey) Ltd *206*
Exeter Hospital Aid Society *181*
Gartmore Fund Managers (Isle of Man) Ltd *204*
MIM Britannia International Ltd *202*
Rothschild Asset Management (CI) Ltd *198*
Target International (Europe) Ltd *196*
TSB Bank *194*


**Relevant Reading from Kogan Page**

*How to Write a Will and Gain Probate*, Marlene Garsia, 1989
*Living and Retiring Abroad: The Daily Telegraph Guide*, 3rd edn, Michael
    Furnell, 1989
*Making Sense of Metric*, 2nd edn, M C D Malcolm, 1989
*Making the Most of Your Retirement*, Keith Hughes, 1989
*Timesharing: A Buyer's Guide*, James Edmonds, 1988
*Working Abroad: The Daily Telegraph Guide*, 12th edn, Godfrey Golzen,
    1989

# Index